HITLER'S ARCTIC WAR

HITLER'S ARCTIC WAR

The German Campaigns in Norway, Finland, and the USSR 1940–1945

CHRIS MANN · CHRISTER JÖRGENSEN

THOMAS DUNNE BOOKS
St. Martin's Press
New York

Copyright © 2002 Brown Partworks Limited
Brown Partworks Limited in part of the Brown Reference
Group

ISBN 0-312-31100-1

First published in the US in 2003 by
St Martin's Press,
175 Fifth Avenue, New York, N.Y.10010

1 3 5 7 9 8 6 4 2

Editorial and design:
Brown Partworks Limited
8 Chapel Place
Rivington Street
London
EC2A 3DQ
UK

Editors: Peter Darman, Tony Hall

Picture Research: Andrew Webb, Nik Cornish

Design: Sandra Horth

Maps: Bob Garwood

Production: Matt Weyland

Printed in Hong Kong

PICTURE CREDITS
Corbis: 35, 191
Robert Hunt Library: 10, 11, 12-13, 14, 15 (both), 16,
17, 18, 19 (both), 20, 24, 25, 26-27, 28, 29, 30, 32-33,
34-35, 36, 37, 38, 39 (both), 40-41, 42, 43, 46, 47, 48-
49, 50, 51, 52, 53, 54-55, 56, 57, 58-59, 61, 62-63, 68,
69, 70-71, 72, 73, 76-77, 78, 79, 82-83, 84, 91, 97, 98-
99, 116-117, 120 (both), 121, 122-123, 124, 125, 126,
127, 130, 131 (both), 132, 133, 135, 138, 142, 143, 144-
145, 146, 147, 148-149, 153, 154-155, 156-157, 186-
187, 188, 189, 192, 194, 195, 196-197, 202-203, 204,
205, 206, 207, 209, 211, 213
Stavka Military Historical Research: 6-7, 64, 65, 66-67,
80-81, 85, 87, 88-89, 92, 92-93, 94-95, 96, 100-101,
102, 102-103, 105, 106, 108, 109, 110-111, 112, 113,
114-115, 136, 137, 140 (both), 141, 150, 151, 158-159,
160, 162, 163, 165, 166, 167, 171, 172, 173, 176, 177,
178, 180, 181, 182, 183, 184, 190, 198, 198-199, 200-201
TRH Pictures: 210

Contents

Maps

Introduction

On land and on the seas, the area around the Arctic Circle is inhospitable. Military operations in this region are difficult, dangerous and place great demands on logistical systems, and also require specially trained soldiers.

The land and seas of the Arctic Circle are among the most inhospitable places on the planet. During World War II, they were a battlefield on a scale beyond anything that region had previously witnessed. The climate in northern Scandinavia is harsh and unforgiving, and makes the most extreme demands on military operations. For example, soldiers must contend with the dangers of the environment as well of those of enemy action. A whole host of physical problems must be faced. In winter, some of the hazards are obvious, such as hypothermia, dehydration, snow blindness and even sunburn. There is also a serious possibility of freezing to death in temperatures that regularly reach minus 40 degrees. The wind-chill factor increases the chance of frostbite, and heat transference may result in flesh sticking to metallic parts of weapons and vehicles. The latter require special oils, higher rates of maintenance, and there is an increased demand for fuel for both heating and transport – engines must be turned over regularly or even kept running constantly. Soldiers operating in these climates also require a higher calorific intake.

All the above burdens a logistical system operating in an area poorly served by communications links. Roads were limited in number and largely of poor quality. As a result, supplies and troops usually had to

Typical terrain in northern Finland and the USSR. For the belligerents in World War II, it was a very demanding environment in which to conduct a military campaign.

Scandinavia and the Baltic, 1939

0 — 300 Miles
0 — 480 Km

North Cape

Banak • Kirkenese
• Alta
Tromso • Skibotn • Petsamo • Murmansk
• Nautsi
Harstad • Kandalaksha
• Narvik
• Muonio

Atlantic Ocean

SWEDEN
• Mosjöen • Rovaniemi
Lulea • Tornio
• Kemi
• Oulu

FINLAND

Namsos •

Trondheim •

Alesund •

Andalsnes •

Hovanger • • Lillehammer
NORWAY • Viipuri
Bergen • HELSINKI • Leningrad
OSLO •
Rjukan • Tallinn
Stavanger • STOCKHOLM • ESTONIA USSR
Arendal •
Egersund • Riga •
Kristiansand • Göteborg • LATVIA

LITHUANIA
Gulf of Bothnia • Memel
COPENHAGEN • Kaunas •
Baltic Sea Danzig • Könisberg
DENMARK E. PRUSSIA
Kiel • • Rostock
Hamburg • POLAND

GERMANY

·············· International boundaries 1/9/39
+–+–+–+ Narvik–Lulea railway

be transported by sea. As to surviving man-made dangers, the frozen ground made digging-in difficult if not impossible. Men fighting in these climes had to be supremely fit, highly trained and well equipped; if they were not they suffered accordingly.[1]

HAZARDS AT SEA

Similarly, the freezing Arctic waters proved a demanding combat environment. The Gulf Stream may keep the sea route via the North Cape open to Murmansk in winter, but the seas it produces are amongst the roughest in the world. The residue of the warm air carried north on the Gulf Stream collides with cold winds blowing southwards from the North Pole. Mixed by the earth's rotation, this produces large depressions, which in turn produce ferocious gales. The huge waves produced when they break on ships soon turn to ice in the freezing air. The ships pitch and roll and take on "green water", which often freezes in contact with cold steel. It builds up into heavy encrustations of thick ice. The accumulations add to the ship's top weight, which causes the ship to consume more oil or coal in her bunkers, thus reducing bottom weight. So stability is reduced and the risk of capsizing is increased. The ice causes deck machinery and weapons to seize. More mundanely, yet no less importantly for the comfort of the crews, conditions aboard, particularly on small ships such as destroyers, the most important combat vessels in these seas in World War II, were miserable given the cold, damp and perpetual motion caused by the high seas. Furthermore, in winter the pack ice moving southwards can narrow the width of the Arctic seas to a mere 128km (80 miles) in places, reducing the chances of making an unnoticed passage. In the summer the perpetual daylight similarly makes location by hostile eyes more likely. The polar seas also produce unique navigational problems. Compasses are affected by the proximity of the North Pole. Even use of the sextant, almanac and chronometer are hampered by the mist, fog, ice and overcast conditions caused by atmospheric depressions. Ships often become lost, and during the war such stragglers were easy prey for enemy submarines. Once sunk or shot down, the chances of survival were extremely limited in seas that seldom reach temperatures above four degrees Celsius. Even if rescued, survival was not guaranteed as there was little understanding of the process of hypothermia in World War II. [2]

Given these conditions, the struggle for the control of the European Arctic and the northern waters around it is a relatively recent phenomena. Of course, Scandinavia had seen more of its fair share of wars in the past. After all, it was home to the Vikings. Through most of sixteenth century the Danes and Swedes struggled for the dominance of the Baltic after the break up of the Kalmar Union. However, the brief Swedish rise to great power status in the following 100 or so years under Gustavus Adolphus and his successors convinced the Danes to renounce the contest, although they would take any advantage thrown up by the seventeenth and eighteenth centuries' many wars. Sweden's main rival became Peter the Great's Russia, and Sweden's hopes of maintaining her Baltic empire disappeared after Charles XII's

The area over which Germany, Finland and the Soviet Union fought their Arctic campaign. It was a theatre that sucked in hundreds of thousands of men over four years of war.

failed march on Moscow in 1708. Despite this, Swedish-Russian rivalry continued through most of the rest of the century. The relatively disastrous experience of the Napoleonic Wars for Denmark and Sweden convinced both nations that maintenance of a low profile was the best course in international relations.[3] Denmark and Sweden left the contest for domination of the Baltic region to Russia and the new rising power, Germany.[4]

By the twentieth century Scandinavia had been relegated to the periphery of Europe politically as well as geographically. Denmark, newly independent Norway and Sweden all relied on a policy of neutrality in international affairs. This served them all well in World War I, and although not untouched by war – all three nations' merchant shipping fleets suffered heavily in the face of German unrestricted submarine warfare – the three countries emerged more or less unscathed. Finland seized the opportunity thrown up by the collapse of Tsarist Russia and the subsequent Bolshevik Revolution and declared her independence. Finland, like her Scandinavian neighbours, put her trust in the newly formed League of Nations for security in the postwar world of the 1920s and 1930s. As the League proved ineffectual in the face of Japanese, Italian and subsequently Nazi German aggression, the Nordic countries stated their strict neutrality and hoped the gathering storm would not break upon them.

The Swedes, and particularly the Finns, with their large Soviet neighbour to the east, looked to improve their defences. The Norwegian Labour and Danish Social

Finnish troops near the front during the Winter War against the USSR. Note their winter camouflage. The gloves were necessary to prevent bare flesh sticking to the frozen metal parts on weapons.

Democrat Governments that dominated the 1930s chose to spend their money elsewhere. The Norwegians provide a suitable example of the ill-preparedness of the Scandinavians in the late 1930s. Field manoeuvres for the army had been cancelled to save costs, and the navy had not left port since 1918 for similar reasons. Equipment was obsolescent at best; money had been put aside to buy a single tank, "so the Norwegian soldiers could see at least one sample in their lifetime". The air force had bought Caproni aircraft from Italy in 1932, not due to their quality but because they could be paid for with dried fish! The Norwegians put their faith in the British Royal Navy to keep the Germans at bay and the Danes, probably rightly, concluded that there was little they could do if Germany decided to invade. In Norway this attitude was maintained despite the fact that Norway's king, Haakon VII, had predicted to the British Admiral Sir John Kelly in 1932 that: "If Hitler comes to power in Germany and manages to hold on to it, then we shall have war in Europe before the decade is out."[5]

Neutrality as a foreign policy is dependent on the maintenance of the balance of power. If that balance tips, small nations, for all their protestations of neutrality, can be very vulnerable if they are strategically important to their aggressive neighbours. As King Haakon so rightly predicted, Hitler becoming dictator in Germany upset the European balance of power and would drag Norway, Denmark and Finland into World War II. Hitler would also turn the Scandinavian peninsula into a battleground for the first time in 125 years, and his war would also bring modern war to the Arctic for the first time. The strategic imperative of the war against Britain would lead to the German invasion of Norway. The great clash between German Nazism and Soviet communism would extend to the far north, and into the freezing seas of the North Cape as the Western Allies tried to supply the embattled Soviet Union.

Adolf Hitler, Nazi dictator of Germany. His decision to secure supplies of Scandinavian iron ore would bring World War II to the Arctic theatre.

Although there is some scholarship on the Norwegian campaign and Arctic convoys, there is little work on Hitler's campaign in the Arctic. This book brings together the wider German involvement in Scandinavia with the specific operations against the Soviets in the vicinity of Murmansk.[6] Christopher Mann has produced a study of Germany's relationship with Finland during the Winter War, the German invasion and occupation of Norway and the Arctic Convoy battles, while Christer Jörgensen has dealt with the German-Soviet struggle of 1941–45. Together they provide a complete account and analysis of Hitler's Arctic War, a struggle which although peripheral, had serious implications for the outcome of World War II.

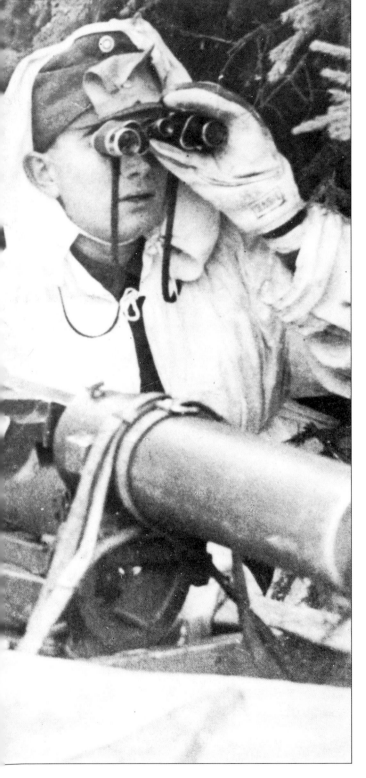

Chapter 1

GERMANY, FINLAND AND THE WINTER WAR

Finland, like other Scandinavian countries, endeavoured to remain neutral in international affairs. However, political changes within Germany and the USSR would lead to the Winter War with the Soviet Union.

World War II came to Scandinavia on 30 November 1939. Like her Scandinavian neighbours Norway and Sweden, Finland had stated her neutrality on the outbreak of war in September 1939, but declarations of neutrality counted for little with Europe's dictators. The Soviet invasion of Finland was a direct consequence of German diplomacy; it is unlikely Stalin would have moved against the Finns without the assurance of German non-intervention

Dressed in winter camouflage uniforms, a Finnish Army machine-gun team prepares to meet a Red Army attack during the Winter War, 8 December 1939.

provided by the Molotov-Ribbentrop Pact of August 1939. However, Germany had long-standing links with Finland, and a Soviet victory would clearly alter the balance of power in the Baltic, perhaps even threaten German iron ore supplies from Sweden, and give the Western Allies (Great Britain and France) an opportunity to dabble in Scandinavian affairs. Hitler's reasons for giving Stalin a free hand in Finland lay largely in the free hand it gave him in the West. The Germans maintained an aloof neutrality in the Winter War, but they noted with interest the performance of the Red Army and their analysis of this would have profound implications for the future. Given the antecedents of German-Finnish relations, this stance might appear strange. German military involvement with Finland dated back to the last years of World War I, and resulted in the establishment of important links between the Finnish and Germany militaries.

Finland had been part of the Russian Empire since 1809. Although initially given considerable autonomy, attempts at Russification in the early twentieth century had caused considerable resentment. So when the Bolshevik coup in Petrograd overthrew the Provisional Government in November 1917, the Finnish leadership saw

Russian Bolshevik leader Lenin (left) hoped that Finland would succumb to a communist revolution and then seek union with Russia. The woman on the right is Lenin's wife.

German troops, part of the Baltic Division, exchange fire with Red forces in Helsinki during the Finnish Civil War.

Russian Commissar for War, Leon Trotsky, urged Finnish socialists to seize power in their own country.

the opportunity to gain their country's independence. On 4 December 1917, Pehr Albin Svinhufvud presented the *Eduskunta*, the Finnish parliament, with what was later called the Declaration of Independence, which was passed two days later.

The new government's main concern was to achieve foreign recognition of Finnish independence. The Germans, who had enjoyed a long period of success against Russia in 1916–17, were keen to foster the separatist tendencies of the nationalities within the Russian Empire, and thereby undermine its ability to fight. So the Germans approved of Finland's actions and the Finns were eager for German support. However, even Germany was unwilling to recognize Finland before Russia did. Sweden, Finland's neighbour, and the rest of Western Europe concurred. Germany therefore insisted that Finland approach Lenin's Bolshevik Government in Petrograd, as clearly this was the only central authority in Russia worth the name. Indeed, the Germans were at the time negotiating with the Bolsheviks for a Russian exit from World War I.

A delegation of Finnish socialists met Lenin on 27 December. He promised to recognize Finnish independence, and the Central Committee of the Bolshevik Party approved his decision in principle the following day. Lenin reasoned that a Finnish revolution would soon follow and his Commissar for War, Leon Trotsky, advised them to take swift action to seize power. The Finnish Government was similarly told that the Bolsheviks would accept Finnish independence, and a delegation headed by Svinhufvud gained Lenin's acceptance on 31 December. This was ratified by the Central Committee on 4 January 1918. Lenin had been forced to deal with the Finnish bourgeois government because the Finnish socialists held similar views on independence. Lenin fully expected that he would soon be dealing with a Finnish workers' government, which, in time no doubt, would request union as a republic in the new Russian Federation of Nations.[1]

Imperial Germany had encouraged the Finns to press for independence, although official recognition did not come until 6 January 1918. German strategy dictated that Finnish territory could be used to further the isolation of Russia. There would, no doubt, be useful trading opportunities too. France had recognized the Finnish declaration two days earlier, desperate not to drive the new nation into German hands. However, France was too cut off from the northeastern Baltic to be of any great use to Finland in the struggle to maintain the latter's fledgling nationhood. Geography, pure and simple, dictated to whom the Finnish Government would have to turn.

A machine-gun company from the Baltic Division advances against Red Guards near Hanko.

General von der Goltz commanded the German Baltic Division in the Finnish Civil War.

The Finnish people, although united in their desire for independence, were less unified in their ideas for Finland's future. The gulf between the bourgeois Finnish Government and the Finnish left grew. The *Eduskunta* granted the government full power to establish an army and restore order, as the country had been racked with strikes and rioting. This was viewed as a direct challenge by the Finnish labour movement, and did much to bring the radicals and moderates on the left together. Both sides began arming rapidly. The gun-running of the left's militia units – the so-called Red Guards – between Viipuri and Petrograd led to full-scale fighting on the Karelian Isthmus on 19 January.[2] The fighting soon spread. On 27–28 January the Red Guards seized Helsinki, and elements of the government managed to flee to Vaasa and set up a rump administration in the White – as the government's forces were known – heartland of Ostrobothnia.

THE FINNISH CIVIL WAR

The Finnish Civil War was a war of frontlines and conventional offensives. The Whites held Northern Finland, Ostrobothnia and Karelia, and the Reds controlled most of the major cities, industrial centres and the south. The country was roughly divided on a line from the Gulf of Bothnia to Lake Ladoga. The size of forces was fairly well matched, probably in the region of 70,000 combatants each, although estimates vary. The Reds were poorly trained, equipped and led for the most part, but had the dubious advantage of the half-hearted support of the Russian troops that remained in Finland. These were more useful as a source of equipment. The Whites had similar deficiencies in training and equipment, and their quality of leadership varied. They were, however, commanded by a number of Tsarist-trained Finnish officers and Swedish volunteers, and were led by one Carl Gustaf Mannerheim, a general who had served in the Imperial Russian Army and was easily the most able commander of the civil war. The one first-class formation available to the Whites was the 27th Jäger Battalion. As part of the wider movement for Finnish independence, a number of Finnish volunteers undertook military training at Lockstedt in Germany under special arrangements with the German authorities. The number of volunteers swelled, and a Jäger (light infantry) battalion was formed as part of the Imperial German Army in May 1916. It saw service in the Kurland area against the Russian Army in 1916–17, but as the situation in Finland worsened the unit returned, landing at Vaasa in February 1918. Mannerheim promptly broke the unit up, thus providing a cadre of experienced officers and noncommissioned officers (NCOs) which he put to work training his army.

Joachim von Ribbentrop, Hitler's Minister for Foreign Affairs. In August 1939 he went to Moscow to finalize the non-aggression treaty with Stalin's Soviet Union.

Although Mannerheim's early campaigns met with success, the war was shortened by German intervention, which the Finnish commander considered unnecessary and undesirable. He accepted that German involvement saved lives, but believed it undermined the achievement of Finnish independence and this motivated him to drive his advance forward as quickly as possible.[3] Two White government officials in Berlin had requested German military aid in early February without official sanction. A week later Germany announced that it would accede to the Finnish request, in effect, inviting itself to the assistance of Finland. On hearing the news, Mannerheim threatened to resign and the government was somewhat perplexed to find itself

Soviet dictator Joseph Stalin (left) with his Foreign Minister Molotov. The latter signed the non-aggression treaty with Nazi Germany on 23 August 1939, thus isolating Finland effectively.

Carl Gustaf Emil Mannerheim, Finnish field marshal, statesman and national hero. Born a Russian national, he rose to the rank of major-general in the Imperial Russian Army.

forced to sign three somewhat disadvantageous agreements: a peace treaty forbidding Finland to deal with other nations without German approval; a trade and maritime agreement granting Germany economic preference; and an undertaking that Finland would pay for the costs of all German military intervention.[4] Even in 1918, Finland was learning that German aid did not come without serious consequences. Given his government's acceptance Mannerheim "loyally bowed to the inevitable."[5] The main German force, General Rüdiger von der Goltz's Baltic Division of some 11,000 men, landed in Finland on 3 April 1918. Three thousand more arrived four days later. The capture of Helsinki followed soon after, and the last major city in Red hands fell on 26 April, with the final surrender occurring in mid-May on the Karelian Isthmus.

Mannerheim had pushed the border with Russia in Karelia eastwards and the unofficial fighting over where the frontier with Bolshevik Russia would lay rumbled on through 1918, 1919 and into 1920. However, Finland's relationship with Germany and her obvious ambitions in the north had serious implications for Finland's relations with the Western Allies. The Germans were pressing the Finns with offers of aid in capturing the rest of Karelia if they helped a German thrust towards the British base at Murmansk (British and Finnish troops had already clashed at Petsamo). Furthermore, the treaties signed with the Germans did more than just place the young state under German patronage, they offered the prospect of German economic penetration that would effectively turn Finland into a German colony.[6] The Finns had also agreed to have a German prince elected king. Inevitably, German influence extended deep into military affairs, and in May 1918 the government had instructed Mannerheim that the army should be reformed along German lines by German officers, essentially handing the responsibility of Finland's defence over to Germany. Mannerheim promptly resigned.

The Russo-German non-aggression treaty allowed Hitler to crush Poland in a three-week campaign. These are German troops in Poland in September 1939.

Until about July 1918, this pro-German policy made considerable sense. Germany was the dominant power in Eastern Europe, and until the failure of the Ludendorff Offensive on the Western Front that month might possibly have emerged victorious. However, Finland's German orientation was rudely brought to an end by the defeat of Imperial Germany by the Western Allies in November 1918. A rapid change in direction had to follow; Prince Friedrich Karl of Hesse renounced his claim to the Finnish throne and the last German troops left Finnish soil in mid-December. The Western Allies were conciliatory, keen to use Finland in their fight against Bolshevik Russia. However, Western recognition of Finnish statehood only followed with the failure of this policy. The Finns were able to conclude a peace with Lenin's government, which was in the midst of the Russo-Polish War and was eager to limit the number of prospective enemies on Russia's borders. The Treaty of Tartu, signed on 14 October 1920, was little more than a settlement of frontiers and certainly did not establish a basis for friendly relations. Indeed, the treaty was probably too advantageous for Finland, placing the border as it did a mere 25km (15 miles) from the outskirts of Petrograd.

RESULTS OF THE FINNISH CIVIL WAR

The results of the Finnish Civil War had serious implications for the future. The war had done much to establish a number of patterns of behaviour which would be the key to Finland's role in the world in the 1920s and 1930s, and in World War II. It did much to cement Finland's animosity towards Russia – not that this was difficult – particularly given the Whites' interpretation of the civil war as a war of liberation against both Russia and such "Red" Russian ideas as Bolshevism. The streak of anti-Russian/anti-Soviet prejudice that ran through many Finnish politicians made accommodation with their much larger neighbour difficult when relations worsened in the late 1930s. Furthermore, the geographical conditions created by the 1920 treaty with Soviet Russia threw up a strategic imperative for the Soviet Union, as a potentially hostile border lay within artillery range of the outskirts of its second city. The war also led to the establishment of a Finnish Army and Mannerheim's impressive military reputation. That army, however, had absorbed German influences and the war had forged links between the Finnish and German militaries. Many men of the Jäger battalion – a formation trained and shaped by the Germans – went on to have successful careers in the Finnish military, perhaps most famously Erik Heinrichs, who commanded the Army of Isthmus during the Winter War.[7] These links were maintained throughout the interwar years, despite the Western orientation of Finland's foreign policy. They would be extremely useful when Finland fought alongside Germany after the invasion of the Soviet Union in June 1941. Conversely, the experience of dealing with the Germans during the civil war seems to have had its influence on Mannerheim, who would prove remarkably adept at keeping them at arm's length, limiting their influence and maintaining Finnish independence even though both countries were engaged in a war against the USSR.

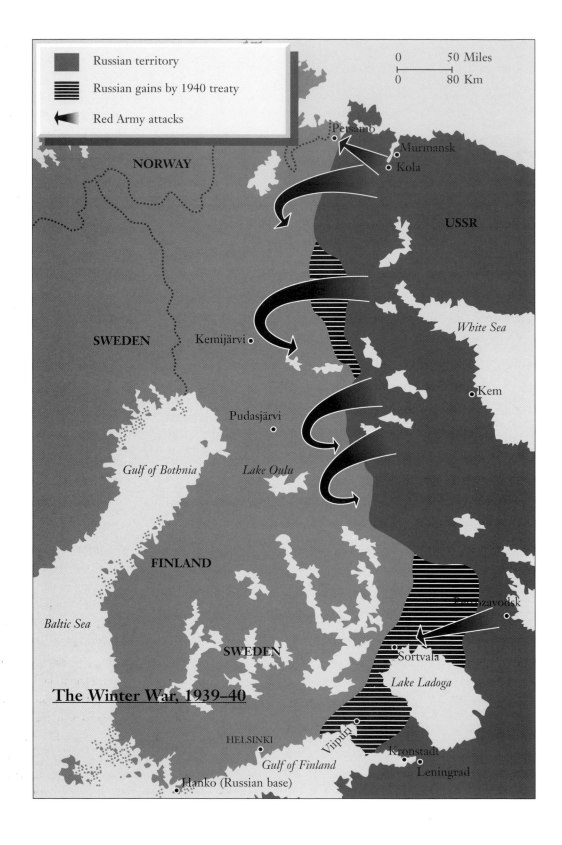

Russian territory

Russian gains by 1940 treaty

Red Army attacks

0   50 Miles
0   80 Km

NORWAY

Petsamo

Murmansk

Kola

USSR

SWEDEN

Kemijärvi

White Sea

Kem

Pudasjärvi

Gulf of Bothnia

Lake Oulu

FINLAND

Baltic Sea

Petrozavodsk

SWEDEN

Sortvala

Lake Ladoga

The Winter War, 1939–40

HELSINKI

Viipuri

Kronstadt

Gulf of Finland

Leningrad

Hanko (Russian base)

Finnish foreign policy in the interwar years was based around a reliance on the League of Nations. However, when it became increasingly clear that League membership was a somewhat ineffectual insurance policy against foreign aggression, the Finns were forced to rely on a strict policy of neutrality. The most important task remained the maintenance of Finnish security against the possible threat of the Soviet Union. Possible allies were few, relations with Sweden were cool, no assurances of assistance from Great Britain and France if the Soviet Union attacked were forthcoming, and so neutrality was the only option. A 10-year non-aggression pact was signed with the Soviet Union in 1932. Yet this was no more an insurance of Soviet good intentions than the similar pacts the USSR signed with Germany and Poland in the same period. However, although relations with the Soviets were strained despite the 1932 treaty, it was not until Nazi Germany's aggressive foreign policy began to undermine the European balance in the late-1930s that Finland's security became seriously threatened.

HITLER AND THE REARMING OF GERMANY

Adolf Hitler became chancellor of Germany in January 1933. Almost at once he set out to rebuild German military power, disregarding the provisions of the 1919 Treaty of Versailles, which forbade German rearmament. Great Britain and France were unwilling to enforce the Versailles settlement, and this seemed equally the case when Germany began to challenge the treaty's territorial clauses. Germany remilitarized the Rhineland in 1936, *Anschluss* (Union) with Austria followed in March 1938 and by the summer of that year Hitler was threatening Czechoslovakia over the Sudetenland. This blatantly aggressive German foreign policy was of serious concern to the Soviet Union. After all, Hitler had made no secret of his dislike of the USSR in *Mein Kampf*, nor in his pronouncements once he gained power.

The Soviet concern was that in an effort to deflect Nazi aggression away from the West, the British might try to direct the Germans northeast into the Baltic region. This idea certainly worried Joseph Stalin, the Soviet dictator, who reckoned that, "[Finland] may well become the springboard for anti-Soviet moves from either of the bourgeois imperialist groupings – the German and Anglo-French-American." He believed that it was possible, "that they are plotting together for joint action against the USSR. Finland might be urged against us as a skirmish for a major war."[8] Strangely, these views were not held by the Soviet Union alone; Sweden also began to worry that Finland might turn to Germany for military help.[9] Although these fears were groundless, it shows that it was not only the USSR that was gripped by paranoia over Finland's possible pro-German orientation.

In mid-April 1938, the second secretary of the Soviet embassy, Boris Yartsev, called on Finnish Foreign Minister Rudolf Holsti.[10] Yartsev warned Holsti that Moscow was convinced of Germany's aggressive intent and that this would impinge on Finnish territory. He said that the Soviet Union sought guarantees that Finland would not

Though the Soviet Union gained territory as a result of the Winter War, the conflict revealed the feeble nature of the Red Army's capabilities, which was not lost on military planners in Berlin.

assist Germany in a future war against the Soviet Union, and that the Soviets would give Finland any help required against Germany. Yartsev was rebuffed. The Soviets tried again through more orthodox channels in April 1939, demanding the lease of certain islands in the Gulf of Finland in return for territory in eastern Karelia. The new Finnish foreign minister Eljas Erkko – Holsti had retired, due to ill health and the fact he had made some offensive remarks about Hitler at a diplomatic dinner in Geneva – again rejected the Soviet proposals.[11] He stated that the Soviet intention to offer automatic help would be "incompatible with the autonomy and sovereignty of Finland", and that Finland would regard "such a measure as aggression."[12] These were harsh words and they added to Soviet unease, given that the independent Baltic states – Latvia, Lithuania and Estonia – were taking a similar stance. To make matters worse General Halder, the Wehrmacht (German Armed Forces) chief of staff,

Finnish troops make use of a wood pile during an exercise. As the Soviets found to their cost, Finland's soldiers were hardy, well-trained foes.

was touring the region. In Finland he inspected the fortifications that the Finns were hurriedly building on the Karelian Isthmus in the wake of Soviet actions.

The Germans had, however, made an approach to Scandinavia that spring, offering Norway, Sweden and Finland non-aggression pacts. This was rejected in May, angering the Germans but not mollifying the Soviets. Nonetheless, Hitler was little bothered by the stance of these countries on the periphery of Europe. His main concern was that he would not have to fight both the Western Allies, Great Britain and France, and the Soviet Union if his aggressive policy towards Poland resulted in war. The Soviets, meanwhile, were disappointed in their efforts to secure close military links with Great Britain and France. So Soviet Foreign Minister Maxim Litvinov was replaced by Vyacheslav Molotov, Stalin's right-hand man and importantly, given the Nazi's rabid anti-Semitism, not Jewish like his predecessor. Stalin was sending a signal to the Germans that having failed to find security in conjunction with the Western powers, he was willing to deal with the Nazis. Joachim von Ribbentrop, the German foreign minister, read the signs correctly and informed Hitler that the Soviets seemed to be considering a military pact with the British and French. This was enough to push Hitler forward. He needed to be sure the Soviets would not oppose his proposed

Finnish troops on patrol during the Winter War. The Finns had excellent winter clothing to protect them from the cold.

invasion of Poland, and he needed an agreement soon so that the Polish campaign could be launched and finished before the winter rains.

Hitler needed to move fast. Friedrich Schulenberg, the German ambassador in Moscow, informed Molotov: "The Reich Government are of the opinion that there is no question between the Baltic Sea and the Black Sea which cannot be settled to the complete satisfaction of both countries", and he requested "a speedy clarification of German-Russian relations."[13] Stalin and Molotov responded cautiously, and it took Hitler's direct intervention to hurry the process along when he telegrammed Stalin on 20 August 1939 asking him to receive von Ribbentrop. This came at just the right time for the Soviet leader, as fighting had broken out with the Japanese for the second year running on the Mongolian-Manchurian frontier. Stalin also feared a two-front war, and to avoid it he was prepared to trust Hitler. By 23 August, von Ribbentrop and Molotov had signed a non-aggression pact. The pact contained a secret protocol dividing Europe into Soviet and German spheres of influence. The Baltic states and Finland were placed in Stalin's sphere. Poland was to be split down the middle and a whole series of economic measures were agreed. For Hitler it meant that he could deal with Poland without Soviet intervention, and once he had finished with the Poles he could turn westwards without concern to his eastern frontiers. For Stalin it meant that he could deal similarly with the Baltic states and Finland if he so chose. Germany's need for a free hand in Poland and, subsequently, the West had sealed Finland's fate. In the late-1930s Finland had been able to shelter under the mutual hostility

of the two main Baltic powers. This balance of power had shifted; Germany and the Soviet Union had come to an understanding, which left Finland highly vulnerable.

It took Hitler little more than a week to act. Germany invaded Poland on 1 September 1939. Great Britain and France declared war on Germany on 3 September. The Scandinavian nations all declared their neutrality. The Western Allies could do little to help the Poles. Serious Polish resistance collapsed in two weeks and the campaign was over in a month. Stalin felt it was time to take what he felt was his own. On 17 September the Red Army occupied much of eastern Poland, and at the beginning of October the Soviets forced Estonia, Lithuania and Latvia to cede military bases to the USSR on their territories. As Mannerheim asked on the fall of Poland: "And whose turn is next, when the appetite of these gentlemen [Hitler and Stalin] has managed to grow?"[14] Finland was to find out very soon. The summons to Moscow to discuss "concrete questions" came on 5 October 1939. The Finnish negotiators headed by Juho Paasakivi were given very little leeway, and on 13 October Paasakivi was forced to reject the Soviet demand for a lease on the port of Hanko as a military base, the movement of the frontier on the Karelian Isthmus westwards by some 70km (43 miles), and cession of certain islands in the Gulf of Finland in return for large areas of Eastern Karelia. A second and third round of talks achieved nothing before discussions broke down irretrievably on 13 November. It was clear Finland could expect no support from outside, while a number of high-ranking Germans had argued that Finland should acquiesce to the Soviet demands. It seems that the Germans were as surprised as most of Europe when the Soviets attacked on 30 November.[15]

THE WINTER WAR BEGINS

Negotiations having failed, Stalin resolved to settle the matter by force. It is clear that he expected the campaign to be over quickly in much the same way as the Germans had defeated Poland. Some officers of the Red Army urged caution, but the prevailing view was that Finland would be defeated in 10 to 12 days.[16] Given the vast disparity in forces this was not an entirely unreasonable assumption. The Finnish Army numbered 30,000 men; it was ill-equipped with regard to modern weapons such as tanks and aircraft. The Soviet commander, General Kirill Meretskov, had 600,000 troops (the Red Army would eventually commit 1,200,000 men), lavishly supported by 1500 tanks and 3000 aircraft.[17] However, the Finns were well led and motivated and familiar with the terrain and conditions. The same cannot be said of the Red Army, whose officer corps had been decimated after Stalin's recent purges.

After a staged border incident, Meretskov's forces rolled over the Finnish frontier in six widely separated advances over a 1400km (868-mile) front. Given the inhospitable nature of most of the frontier, the Finnish commander-in-chief, Mannerheim, was able to concentrate the bulk of his forces on the Karelian Isthmus. Here, 20,000 men dug-in behind the Mannerheim Line – a series of fieldworks stretching across the isthmus – managed to hold the main weight of the Soviet advance, some 180,000

Finnish soldiers examine Russian dead during the Winter War. The Red Army suffered 126,875 killed in four months of fighting in attacks against the Mannerheim Line.

men, throughout December without forcing Mannerheim to commit his reserves. After 27 December the Soviets broke off this offensive. The Soviet push north of Lake Ladoga was larger than Mannerheim had anticipated, and he was forced to draw on his reserves to stabilize the situation. In the far north the Soviets easily captured the port of Petsamo but failed to push farther south. By late December the Finns were able to move on to the offensive: spectacular victories were secured by Colonel Talvela at Tolvajärvi on 24 December and Colonel Siialasvuo at Suomassalmi in early January, where with the strength of roughly a brigade he destroyed two crack Soviet divisions. These successes convinced some in the Finnish Government that the war was winnable, although Mannerheim was always aware that the strategic situation remained grim. However, these events did at least provoke a change in Soviet political and military policy.

The Soviets abandoned their plan to put in place a puppet regime under the veteran Finnish communist Otto Kuusinen, and continuous contact was established between the two governments from 29 January 1940. The Finnish bargaining position was strengthened by the interest that Great Britain and France were now taking in the conflict. The Western Allies had at once condemned the Soviet invasion and were much heartened by the difficulties in which the Red Army found itself. Indeed, the British also hoped that the Finnish-Soviet War, or Winter War, might also embarrass the Germans. To quote

Finnish troops on watch during the Winter War. Thanks to training and good clothing, cases of frostbite were virtually unknown among Finnish soldiers.

the British ambassador in Paris, Oliver Harvey, "no German except an absolute extremist can feel anything but acute discomfort at seeing the Russians attack the Finns – the Nordic race par excellence – whose independence was originally won by German aid."[18]

The British and French had expected a German offensive on the Western Front within weeks of the outbreak of war. When it failed to materialize, they found themselves looking to Scandinavia as a means to break the deadlock. Germany obtained well over half its iron ore imports from northern Sweden. There was a "growing belief in Swedish iron ore as the Achilles' heel of the German war economy."[19] The unexpectedly resolute Finnish resistance to the Soviets provided the Allies with the opportunity to intervene in Scandinavia, and block Swedish iron ore supplies to Germany under the pretext of aiding the Finns. In early February 1940, the British and French Governments decided to send an expeditionary force to Scandinavia, ostensibly to help Finland. However, this force would land at Narvik in Norway, and seize the iron ore mines in northern Sweden before providing any military support to the Finns. This plan required at the very least the acquiescence of the Norwegians and Swedes, which was extremely unlikely, given the two countries' determined neutrality. British preparations went ahead throughout February and early March 1940. However, activation of the plan required an appeal by Finland for help.

Finnish ski troops such as these inflicted many casualties on the Red Army during the Winter War. Frostbite and hunger added to the Soviets' woes.

The Finns were desperate for military materiel, and although the free world expressed its admiration and sympathy for Finland, very little practical aid was forthcoming. Sweden, although refusing to intervene in the war, did at least sell Finland considerable quantities of arms and supplies, and allowed some 8000 men to volunteer to fight for Finland. Germany, however, remained strictly neutral. This was very much in line with Hitler's belief that Germany would not become involved in a Soviet-Finnish war. Indeed, he was somewhat scornful:

"I have no great regard for countries of the North. Ever since I came to power, the papers of Sweden, Norway and Finland have vied with one another in insulting me personally . . . I have truly no reason to feel any friendship towards countries whose press have treated me with such indignity. As for Finland, seeing that Germany in 1918, through Von der Goltz's expedition, helped Finland out of a difficult spot, I should think that we are entitled to expect greater gratitude and consideration than we have been accorded."[20]

The Germans had even blocked the passage of Italian aid to the Finns and refused to even honour Finnish arms orders placed before the outbreak of war. When the new Finnish foreign minister,

Soviet Marshal Semyon Timoshenko was given substantial reinforcements with which to breach the Mannerheim Line.

Väino Tanner, questioned the German minister in Helsinki, Wipert von Blücher, he similarly criticized Finland for its ingratitude regarding 1918 and its current "downright unfriendly" attitude towards Germany. He warned Tanner that Germany would not allow the Allies to secure bases in the north and that such a concession would be a *casus belli* for Germany. Otherwise, Germany's attitude was, "Germany has no part in the Finnish War."[21] He certainly rejected Tanner's suggestion that Germany might approach the Soviet Union with regards to opening peace negotiations.

SOVIET VICTORY IN THE WINTER WAR

Meanwhile, the Soviets had also reorganized their military capabilities. Meretskov was replaced by the far more capable Semyon Timoshenko. The Red Army was reinforced, and an intensive training programme was developed using close cooperation between infantry, tanks, artillery and aircraft. During late February and early March 1940, Timoshenko delivered mass tank, air and artillery attacks on the Mannerheim Line until he broke it. Once through, he made for Viipuri, which he captured on 11 March. Mannerheim, seeing the position was hopeless, advised the government to make peace. The Finns debated whether to accept British and French aid, but rightly considered such help would be of extremely limited value and thus sued for peace. A delegation flew to Moscow and signed the peace treaty on 12 March 1940. Hostilities ceased the following day. The Finns were forced to cede the Karelian Isthmus, their second city of Viipuri, areas west and north of Lake Ladoga and a 30-year lease on the Hanko Peninsula to the USSR. The Winter War was over.

The implications of the Winter War were serious for Scandinavia. The Anglo-French intervention plan had drawn Hitler's attention to their evident interest in the north. He therefore ordered plans for a full-scale invasion of Norway. As to the results of the war, there were two key issues. The Soviet Union had won a dangerous victory. Finland was deeply embittered and extremely hostile towards its Soviet neighbour, and would take the first opportunity to have its revenge. Thus Finland would react positively when Hitler suggested a new war against the Soviets, some 18 months later. Without the Winter War, Germany would have still invaded the Soviet Union in 1941, but the invasion would have been planned differently and would not have included the Finns.

Secondly, the poor performance of the Soviet troops gave Hitler the impression that the Red Army could easily be defeated. A German general staff evaluation of late December 1939, prepared after its failed offensive, concluded that the Red Army, "was in quantity a gigantic military instrument . . . leadership itself, however, too young and inexperienced . . . The Russian 'mass' is no match for an army with modern equipment and superior leadership."[22] Or, as put somewhat more colourfully by Swedish historian Christer Jörgensen, "the war gave Hitler the fatal impression that the Red Army was rotten to the core and led by military blockheads."[23] Thus Hitler and the Wehrmacht would seriously underestimate the Soviet Union's ability to resist when he invaded in June 1941.

Chapter 2

THE INVASION
OF NORWAY

The German invasion of Norway was a daring use of land, sea and air power. The Germans quickly overran Norway's paltry defences and then defeated British and French troops that were landed in the north of the country.

The Finnish-Soviet Winter War briefly shifted the world's attention to Scandinavia. Although British and French plans to break the deadlock of the "Phoney War" in the West by intervening had come to nothing, their evident interest in the region led Hitler to order the invasion of Denmark and Norway in an effort to forestall any future Allied plans. The German invasion was a spectacular tactical success. It was a brilliantly executed campaign, in which the Germans showed a remarkable grasp of operations in "three dimensions, land, sea and air."[1] Indeed, it is arguable that the German invasion of Norway was the first proper "combined-arms" operation. It was also Hitler's first land victory against the Western Allies. The British, French and Norwegians were comprehensively defeated, but not without inflicting serious losses on the Germans, particularly to the

German troops in action in Norway on 24 April 1940. The bipod-mounted weapon is an MG 34 machine gun, which had a cyclic rate of fire of 900 rounds a minute.

Kriegsmarine, the German Navy, which would have crucial strategic implications for the rest of the war.

One of the few books Hitler read on naval strategy was Vice Admiral Wolfgang Wegener's *The Sea Strategy of the World War*, which was published in 1929. Wegener's thesis was that the German High Seas Fleet in World War I should have challenged its restriction to the southern part of the North Sea imposed by the British Royal Navy. The British had imposed a Scotland–Bergen blockade, which was facilitated by a sympathetic but ostensibly neutral Norway. Wegener concluded that the blockade could have been broken by the swift occupation of Norway, where the German Navy could have established useful strategic bases.[2]

The outbreak of war in September 1939 was viewed with considerable pessimism by the Commander-in-Chief of the Kriegsmarine, Grand Admiral Erich Raeder. He had been assured by Hitler that war with Great Britain and France would not occur until 1944, by which time the German Navy would be in a position seriously to

Vidkun Quisling (right), the founder of the Norwegian fascist Nasjonal Samling. He was made puppet prime minister of Norway by Hitler.

National Socialist ideologist Alfred Rosenberg (below) introduced Quisling to the commander of the German Navy, Erich Raeder, in December 1939.

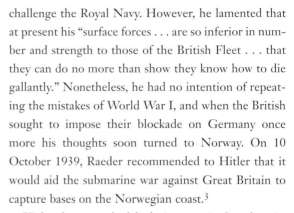

challenge the Royal Navy. However, he lamented that at present his "surface forces . . . are so inferior in number and strength to those of the British Fleet . . . that they can do no more than show they know how to die gallantly." Nonetheless, he had no intention of repeating the mistakes of World War I, and when the British sought to impose their blockade on Germany once more his thoughts soon turned to Norway. On 10 October 1939, Raeder recommended to Hitler that it would aid the submarine war against Great Britain to capture bases on the Norwegian coast.[3]

Hitler, however, had little interest in Scandinavia. His main concern was the forthcoming campaign in the West. Raeder's concerns were no more than a distraction from the more serious business in hand, and he therefore turned down the admiral's proposal. Raeder tried again on 8 December and received the same answer. However, a way soon appeared to change the Führer's thinking. The Nazi political theorist, Alfred Rosenberg, suggested that Raeder should meet his Norwegian protégé, Vidkun Quisling, head of a peripheral but vocal extreme right-wing party in Norway, the *Nasjonal Samling* (NS – National Unity). Raeder readily accepted. For Quisling this was an opportunity to gain support for the NS from the German Navy, while the British threat – now manifesting itself in the Anglo-French plan to intervene in the Finnish-Soviet War – was his trump card. Raeder, keen to further his plans for naval bases in Norway, and Rosenberg, who had envisaged the incorporation of racially "pure" Norway into the Greater Reich, therefore ensured Quisling received an audience with Hitler.[4] In fact, Hitler was interested enough in Quisling to meet him twice, on 14 and 18 December. Hitler's basic position was that he would prefer Norway to remain neutral, but to reassure Quisling concerning the Norwegian's fears of a British violation of Norwegian neutrality, he claimed that he would land in Norway with six, eight, twelve divisions, and even more if necessary, to beat the British to the post. He was much in favour of Norwegian neutrality, but if ever he detected the slightest British intention of entering Norway, he promised to intervene.

Hitler ordered a study of a possible invasion codenamed *Studie Nord*, and General Jodl, the Chief of Operations at the Oberkommando der Wehrmacht (OKW – Armed Forces High Command), noted that it should be carried out with the "smallest possible staff". It was obviously a largely theoretical exercise, as Hitler was emphatic in his insistence that he felt a neutral Norway was in Germany's best interest.

The OKW had a first draft ready on 20 January 1940, and Hitler ordered the establishment of a Sonderstab (special staff) to prepare operational plans for what was now codenamed *Weserübung* (Weser Exercise). Nonetheless, even though planning continued apace, it was clear the process remained academic, as Admiral Kranke of the Sonderstab later noted: "I was under the impression that [Hitler and Jodl] were not firmly resolved to execute the operation." This somewhat benevolent attitude changed overnight with the boarding by the Royal Navy of the *Altmark*, the supply ship of the pocket battleship *Graf Spee* – which had been scuttled in the River Plate on 17 December 1939 – and the liberation of 303 Allied merchant seaman held on board in Jössingfjord, Norway, on 14 February 1940. Hitler was outraged and Raeder noted that: "The event threw a whole new light on the matter for it showed that the Oslo government was no longer capable of enforcing its neutrality." [5]

OKW planning suddenly gained new impetus as Hitler was now convinced that the British were about to intervene in Norway. "Equip ships, put units in readiness," he demanded of Jodl, who calmly replied that no commander for the expedition had yet been appointed. General Keitel, the chief of the OKW, suggested General Nikolaus von Falkenhorst, and he was summoned to see the Führer on 20 February.[6] Von Falkenhorst had served with von der Goltz in Finland in 1918, and this apparently qualified him for operations in the north. When he met the Führer the following day, Hitler asked him about his experiences in Finland, told the general that a British invasion of Norway was expected imminently, and sent him off to come up with an outline plan. Hitler was convinced that Allied dominance in Scandinavia would open up the Baltic Sea and Germany's undefended Baltic coast to the Royal Navy, and cut Germany off from the vital Swedish iron ore. Keitel believed that von Falkenhorst had been summoned to Berlin merely to be sounded out, but Hitler either got carried away or decided that he had found his man. Whatever the case, Hitler seems to have made a very firm decision. He gave von Falkenhorst a rough idea of what he wanted. Falkenhorst was told he had five divisions at his disposal, and that only the major ports need be captured. Hitler wanted to see his ideas that evening.

Von Falkenhorst promptly, "went to town and bought a *Baedeker*, a tourist guide, in order to find out what Norway was like . . . I had no idea; I wanted to

German Gebirgsjäger (mountain troops) on parade (opposite). The 3rd Gebirgs Division spearhead the German attack on Norway.

Grand Admiral Erich Raeder supported an invasion of Norway.

know where the ports were, how many inhabitants Norway had, and what kind of country this was . . . I absolutely did not know what to expect."[7] He returned to Hitler at five, had his plan approved and was told to get on with the detailed planning.

Von Falkenhorst selected his staff from XXI Corps, which he had commanded prior to this assignment, with the addition of naval experts such as Admiral Kranke. It was an extraordinary break with standard German practice that a corps headquarters, the lowest level in the command structure, should be planning an operation that would under normal circumstances be given to an army or army group headquarters. However, Hitler wanted to keep *Weserübung* out of the hands of the Oberkommando der Heeres (OKH – Army High Command), in which he had little trust. Essentially the invasion of Norway was OKW responsibility.[8] Von Falkenhorst's plan built on Kranke's

Franz Halder, Chief of the General Staff of the German Army, was kept on the fringes of the planning for the invasion of Norway.

Sonderstab work and added some innovations of its own. The most significant was the occupation of Denmark as a stepping stone to Norway and to provide forward air bases for the Luftwaffe (German Air Force). In its essentials, however, it was an audacious if straightforward operation. The first echelon would consist of six groups attacking the six main objectives:

Group I: "Narvik", consisting of 2000 men of the 3rd Gebirgs (Mountain) Division transported by 10 destroyers and escorted by the battle cruisers *Scharnhorst* and *Gneisenau*.

Group II: "Trondheim", with 1700 men carried by four destroyers escorted by the heavy cruiser *Admiral Hipper*.

Group III: "Bergen", with 1300 men aboard two destroyers escorted by the light cruisers *Köln* and *Königsberg*.

Groups IV and V: "Kristiansand" and "Egersund", with the cruiser *Karlsruhe*, the depot ship *Tsing Tau*, three torpedo boats and four minesweepers.

Group VI: "Oslo", with the spearhead of the 163rd Division, the operation's general staff and elements such as the Gestapo, aboard the cruisers *Blücher*, *Lützow* and *Emden* and escorted by three destroyers.

On 28 February Hitler approved the plan but a number of problems arose. *Weserübung* would not be allowed to clash with Plan *Gelb*, the offensive in the West. Von Falkenhorst was therefore heavily restricted in the number of airborne troops he could deploy (only four companies of paratroopers with one airborne regiment in reserve), while General Halder, the OKH chief of staff, who was largely unaware of what was going on, only grudgingly released the mountain troops von Falkenhorst

Alfred Jodl (opposite above) was Chief of Operations at OKW, the office that handled the Norwegian invasion plans.

General Nikolaus von Falkenhorst (opposite below) planned the German invasion of Norway.

requested. The portly commander of the Luftwaffe, Hermann Göring, was enraged that airborne units had been placed under von Falkenhorst's command, but his protests to Hitler were to no avail. The navy at least was more enthusiastic.

On 3 March Hitler decided to launch *Weserübung* before *Gelb*. As the British and French frantically tried to persuade Finland to accept their aid in the days before the Finns signed the ceasefire with the Soviets, Hitler considered launching the operation early to forestall the Allies. The Peace of Moscow between the Finns and Soviets, however, allowed preparations to continue at a calmer pace, and on 7 March Hitler formally authorized the use of land forces in the operation. Four infantry divisions – the 69th, 163rd, 181st and 196th – the 3rd Gebirgs Division and the 11th Motorized Rifle Brigade were assigned to Norway (the 11th Motorized Rifle Brigade was later replaced by the 214th Infantry Division). Denmark would be attacked by the 170th, 198th and 214th Infantry Divisions under General Kaupisch. The airborne element, as mentioned, was a mere four companies of the 7th Air Division.[9] The X Air Corps was to provide air support and transport. It was at this late stage that the winding down of Allied plans in Scandinavia removed the operation's justification, and Jodl and Raeder expressed their doubts, but moral justifications rarely bothered Adolf Hitler. Both Raeder and Jodl soon overcame their reservations and supported Hitler's decision of 2 April to set "Weser Day" for 9 April.

Oddly enough, the British determination to halt Swedish iron ore did not die with the failure to aid Finland.[10] Winston Churchill, the First Lord of the Admiralty, remained resolved to halt the sea passage of ore supplies from the Norwegian port of Narvik southwards to Germany within the Norwegian Leads (the Baltic route from southern Swedish ports that were blocked by ice during the winter). To force the German ore ships out into the open sea, where they might be prey to the Royal Navy, he advocated the mining of Norwegian territorial waters. The British

The German heavy cruiser Blücher *was sunk by a single Norwegian shell that landed in the middle of her ammunition hold.*

Admiralty was authorized to mine the Leads on 8 April. Churchill named the operation "Wilfred", "because by itself it was so small and innocent."[11] As a result, considerable Royal Navy units set out for the Norwegian coast on 8 April, but by then the German invasion fleet had already sailed.

Early on the morning of 7 April Admiral Lütjens, the naval commander of *Weserübung*, ordered his flagship, *Gneisenau*, to leave Wilhelmshaven with the rest of Group I for Narvik while Group II headed for Trondheim. These were not the first German ships to sail, however. Seizing all Norway's major ports, some as far north as the Arctic Circle, in a single move meant that although the entire first wave of troops were carried aboard warships, the lighter warships, such as destroyers, would have to be refuelled. Furthermore, supplies and heavy equipment needed to be carried by transports. Both tankers and transports were slower, and thus in order to synchronize their moves some elements had sailed even earlier, between 3 and 6 April.

Lütjens' force was spotted by Royal Air Force (RAF) Coastal Command aircraft that morning, but the British Admiralty did not believe that the German ships were heading for Norway. Rather, it was believed that the capital ships were intending to break out into the Atlantic and attack merchant shipping.[12] To counter this, the British Home Fleet sailed from its base at Scapa Flow and headed northeast in an effort to block the presumed German move towards the Atlantic. Nonetheless, the 2nd Cruiser Squadron, under Vice-Admiral Edward-Collins, was ordered to patrol an area off the Norwegian coast north of Stavanger. By that time, however, Group I was north of this position. Admiral Sir Charles Forbes, Commander of the Home Fleet, might have still caught Group II heading for Trondheim or Group III which had not yet sailed, but he was expecting a German breakout into the Atlantic and, in British terms, that was strategically more important.

Although Groups I and II had enjoyed considerable luck thus far, the destroyers struggled to maintain the speed of 26 knots set by *Gneisenau*, and by the morning of 8 April were scattered. One does not need to dwell too long on the conditions below decks for the 200 troops aboard each vessel. The destroyer *Hans Lüdemann* had become separated from Group I and made chance contact with the British destroyer HMS *Glowworm*, which similarly was separated from the British battlecruiser *Renown*, undertaking a mining

operation in the vicinity of Vestfjord. A desultory running battle followed as Captain Friedrichs of the *Hans Lüdemann* rightly considered that his priority was to deliver his passengers to Narvik. Another lost German destroyer, the *Bernd von Armin*, blundered on to the scene and soon found herself the *Glowworm*'s main quarry. Captain Rechel signalled for assistance and fortunately for the *Armin*, Group II's heavy cruiser, *Admiral Hipper*, was nearby. In theory the contest between the 10,160-tonne (10,000-ton) *Hipper* and the 1366-tonne (1345-ton) *Glowworm* should have been extremely one-sided to say the least, but the British ship held out long enough to relay the position of the German fleet and, after being terribly damaged and having used up all her torpedoes, in an act of extraordinary courage and determination rammed the *Hipper*, tearing a 39.5m (130ft) gash down her starboard side before being sunk.[13] Captain Heye of the *Hipper* managed, however, to get his ship safely into Trondheim despite a four-degree list. The first shots of the Norwegian campaign had been fired.

The *Glowworm*'s message led the Admiralty to order Admiral Whitworth aboard *Renown* to prevent any German ships entering Vestfjord. Whitworth began to concentrate his forces in open seas on the evening of the 8th. This enabled Commodore Bonte to lead his German destroyer flotilla past him and into Narvik with much skill, and not a little luck given the appalling weather. However, Whitworth did by chance clash with Bonte's escorts, *Scharnhorst* and *Gneisenau*, as they sailed for open sea, in

The German heavy cruiser Admiral Hipper *engages the British destroyer HMS* Glowworm *on 8 April 1940. The British ship was sunk in the fight.*

the early hours of 9 April. The *Renown* gained a number of hits on *Gneisenau* but subsequently lost touch with Lütjens, who was not eager to continue the fight despite his superior firepower, and so contact was not re-established. Whitworth ordered his destroyers back to Vestfjord, but by then Narvik was already in German hands. Indeed, this pattern had been repeated everywhere. The German groups had evaded the Home Fleet, and by dawn on 9 April were in position off Narvik, Trondheim, Stavanger, Bergen, Egersund and Oslo.

Only now were the Norwegians waking up to the fact that a German invasion of their country was under way. The Norwegian Admiralty had received news of a vast armada of German ships passing Denmark, but when questioned the German naval attaché in Oslo claimed that he "supposed the fleet had sailed to protect the German coast . . . Until late in the evening of 8 April both the [Norwegian] government and general staff at the Admiralty remained entirely ignorant of the whole operation. Actually no one expected it."[14]

This was not entirely the case. Since 5 April Colonel Hatledal, the Norwegian Army chief of staff, alarmed by the reports emanating from Berlin and Copenhagen,

The light cruiser Emden *was part of the German force that attempted to capture Oslo by surprise.*

had been pressing for mobilization. It had been to no avail. Not that the Norwegian armed forces, even fully mobilized, were that formidable. The Labour Party government that had dominated the political scene had placed its spending priorities elsewhere, and much of the army, navy and air force's equipment was at best obsolescent, as well as being utterly deficient in terms of armour, anti-tank weaponry and modern fighter aircraft. In theory, the six-division army on mobilization should have been 56,000 men, expanded to an absolute maximum of 106,000 men with the addition of territorial units.[15] Full-scale mobilization had never been practised, and even field manoeuvres had been abolished to save money. Given Hatledal's lack of success in urging mobilization and the country's general state of unreadiness, the Norwegians were able to put nowhere near this number of men in the field.

NORWEGIAN INEPTITUDE

Shortly before 11:30 hours, two coastal defence forts at the mouth of Oslofjord reported that a number of foreign ships of unknown nationality were entering the fjord. Hatledal alerted the Commander-in-Chief of the Army, General Laake, and the government. As the cabinet assembled it learned that ships had also appeared off Bergen and that these vessels were German. Extraordinarily, the government ordered only partial mobilization and that the call-up notices should be sent by post! Meanwhile the Norwegian foreign minister, Halvdan Koht, was being presented with a demand for total and unconditional capitulation by the German diplomat Kurt Bräuer to avoid "entirely useless bloodshed". The Norwegian Government rejected the German note unanimously. Bräuer responded when informed of the decision at about 05:30 hours on 9 April that: "There will be fighting and nothing can save you." But as Koht pointed out, the shooting had already started.[16]

The German troops of General Eduard Dietl's mountain division were relieved to enter the calmer inshore waters of Oforfjord, which leads to Narvik's port. The 2160km (1200-mile) journey had been undertaken in terrible weather and the troops had been chilled, soaked and wracked with seasickness. To quote one of them, Franz Püchler: "The sea was so rough that our quarters were in a terrible mess. Everything that was not nailed or screwed down had been flung about . . . Sleep was out of the question."[17] The *Diether von Röder* remained outside the fjord as a guard. At the mouth of the fjord, Commodore Bonte believed that there were two small fortresses, and so he detached the *Hans Lüdemann* and the *Anton Schmitt* with their troops to deal with the Norwegian positions. It turned out German intelligence was wrong and that these were only half-built and unmanned blockhouses. He detached three more ships up Herjangsfjord to capture the army supply depot at Elvesgård, which surrendered without a shot being fired.

Bonte sailed into the harbour with his three remaining vessels, *Wilhelm Heidkamp*, *Bernd von Armin* and *Georg Thiele*. Here at last he met some opposition – the two coastal defence ships the *Eidsvold* and the *Norge*. These ancient vessels dated from

The German invasion of Norway was a daring operation that skillfully combined air, land and naval elements to overwhelm the Norwegians and their British and French allies.

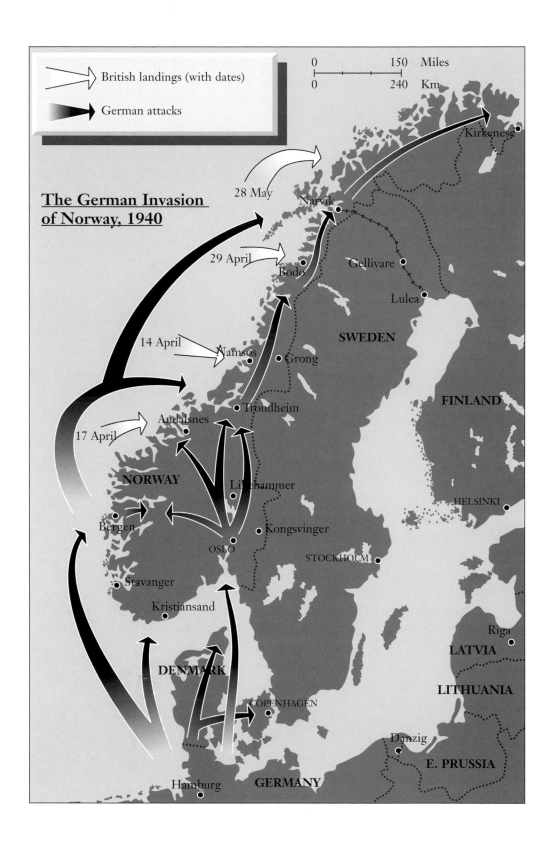

British landings (with dates)

German attacks

0   150   Miles

0   240   Km

The German Invasion of Norway, 1940

Kirkenese

28 May

Narvik

29 April

Bodo

Gellivare

Lulea

SWEDEN

14 April

Namsos

Grong

FINLAND

Trondheim

Andalsnes

17 April

NORWAY

Lillehammer

HELSINKI

Bergen

Kongsvinger

OSLO

Stavanger

STOCKHOLM

Kristiansand

Riga

LATVIA

DENMARK

LITHUANIA

COPENHAGEN

Danzig

E. PRUSSIA

Hamburg

GERMANY

With Oslo secured, the Germans could reinforce their forces in Norway. These troops have just been landed at Oslo harbour, 24 April 1940.

Troops aboard a German ship wait to disembark during the invasion of Norway.

1900. The *Eidsvold* fired a warning shot across the *Hiedkamp*'s bow. Bonte sent an emissary across to the Norwegian ship who, when his request that the Germans be allowed to enter the harbour was refused, calmly stepped off the *Eidsvold* and fired a red Very cartridge, at which signal the *Hiedkamp* sent four torpedoes into the aged vessel, sending it to the bottom with most its crew. The *Norge* at least had some warning, and was able to engage the *Armin* as it was tying up at the Post Peer. However, its poor gunnery allowed Captain Rechel to put a couple of torpedoes into the *Norge*, after which the German commander resumed landing his troops. The Norwegian military response at Narvik was even less effective: the commander of a battalion of the 13th Infantry Regiment, Colonel Sundlo, surrendered unconditionally within in an hour without firing a shot. General Dietl could report to von Falkenhorst in Hamburg by 08:10 hours that Narvik was completely in German hands.

At Trondheim things went even smoother for the Germans. The forts guarding the approach were taken completely by surprise and fired hopelessly at the passing

German ships. Three destroyers and the troops were detached to deal with the forts, while the *Hipper* and a single destroyer raced for the harbour. Two companies of the 138th Mountain Regiment detached from the 3rd Gebirgs Division, under Colonel Weiss, were enough to secure the town's immediate capitulation. Then the *Hipper* turned back to help deal with the coastal defence forts, which had succeeded in seriously damaging one of the German destroyers. It took two days to subdue the

German troops at Narvik on 9 April 1940. Soon after this photograph was taken the British sank this unidentified destroyer.

stubborn resistance of the men manning these forts, but it was to little purpose given that Trondheim itself had fallen without a shot. The small airfield at Vaernes, 32km (20 miles) northeast of Trondheim, held out until the following day.

Admiral Schumdt's Group III narrowly missed the British Home Fleet off Stavanger, and was outside Korsfjord which leads to Bergen, Norway's second city, on schedule by 02:00 hours. He dropped a small force from General Tittel's 69th Infantry Division to deal with the fort at Kvaren, but so tight was the schedule that he had to push on past the Norwegian position before it was captured. The battery managed to score hits on the *Bremse* and *Karl Peters* and inflict serious damage on the light cruiser *Königsberg* before they broke through the coastal defences. The fort was finally taken after a Luftwaffe attack. The Norwegian troops in Bergen, however, quickly withdrew in good order, allowing the *Köln* to land her troops who soon secured the city.

THE FIGHT FOR KRISTIANSAND

Group IV had considerable problems in entering Kristiansand harbour. Although the small town of Arendal was easily taken under cover of fog, Captain Rieve of the *Karlsruhe* found that the fog had hidden the entrance to the fjord. In the improving light the fortress on the island on Odderöy opened fire with such accuracy that Rieve was forced to retreat. He then called for air support. At 07:00 hours he tried again in the wake of a Luftwaffe air raid and was no more successful. The captain then attempted to get the troops of the 163rd Division ashore by torpedo boat, but he was thwarted by the fog again, and in the process all but ran the *Karlsruhe* aground. Finally he resorted to subterfuge, and at 11:00 hours the Norwegian fortress received a message in Norwegian code: "British and French destroyers coming to your help. Do not fire." It was a deception tactic much used by the Germans on 9 April. As the Germans tried again the Norwegian guns remained silent as they tried to identify the fog-shrouded warships. Apparently recognizing the French tricolour, the Norwegians allowed them to pass and Rieve was finally able to occupy the town 12 hours behind schedule.[18] The Group VI operation against the cable station at Egersund was a very much more minor affair, and 150 cyclists of the 69th Division easily captured their objective.

Central to the German plan was the capture of a number of airfields, which would be vital for the projection of German air power in the later stages of the campaign. Sola airfield near Stavanger was strafed by Messerschmitt Bf 110s at around 09:30 hours, and these were followed by 11 Junkers Ju 52 transports led by Captain Gunther Capito, each of which dropped 12 paratroopers. They soon routed the Norwegian platoon guarding the airfield, although they suffered some loses to Norwegian machine-gun fire. In the following days, 180 Ju 52s flew in roughly 2000 troops of the 69th Division, who soon secured Stavanger, while three German sea transports landed the division's 193rd Regiment.

A similar coup de main was planned for Fornebu at Oslo, but the naval operations there did not go to plan. Group V had been spotted by British submarines and had suffered a bruising, if one-sided, encounter with the Norwegian armed trawler *Pol III*. A number of troops were dropped off by the minesweepers and torpedo boats to capture the forts at Rauöy and Bolaerene. The same force then moved against the naval base at Horten. However, the main defences in Oslofjord still lay ahead. The main convoy approached the 457m (500yd) channel through the Dröbak narrows, in front of Fort Oscarborg, led by the heavy cruiser *Blücher*. The garrison commander, aware of the age and inaccuracy of his 280mm guns, opened fire on the German ship at point-blank range causing serious damage. It was then hit by two torpedoes from land-based tubes at Kaholmen. At 07:30 hours an explosion in the magazine of her secondary armament capsized the *Blücher*. One thousand men went down with her, including 600 men of the 163rd Infantry Division and most of the headquarters staff. Captain Thiele of the *Lützow* took command, but not before his ship had taken three hits. He withdrew the remainder of the group and disembarked the troops to storm the enemy positions, and ordered the rest to make their way to Oslo by road. Despite repeated air attacks the forts held out until the following day, and only then was Oslofjord deemed safe for German ships. The capture of Oslo was now seriously behind schedule.

British and French troops in northern Norway in April 1940. In general, Allied aid to the Norwegians was haphazard and inadequate.

French Alpine troops make a dramatic landing in Norway from a ship. Their performance in battle in Norway was less spectacular.

Things nearly went as disastrously at the airfield at Fornebu just outside Oslo. The plan had required the seizure of the airfield by paratroopers dropped by Lieutenant Martin Drewes' Kampfgeschwader (bomber group) 1, where they would be met by Captain Spiller, the German air attaché. They would be followed 20 minutes later by Captain Richard Wagner's Group 103, which would land an infantry battalion. They were escorted by Lieutenant Werner Hansen's Zerstörer Geschwader (Destroyer Squadron) 76 of eight Bf 110s.[19] However, the fog was bad over the Skagerrack and the squadron carrying the paratroopers was forced to turn back. Göring had ordered that if the paratroopers failed to capture Fornebu, the rest of the force must turn back and the commander of X Air Corps, General Geisler, therefore ordered Wagner to abort the mission.

Wagner, however, ignored the order and pressed on. Hansen, commanding the Bf 110s, was already over Fornebu and brushed off the challenge of a handful of Norwegian Gladiator biplanes which had managed to get into the air. He did not know that the paratroopers had returned to Germany. Eventually, Wagner's planes arrived and he made the first approach onto the airfield, but his aircraft were hit by ground fire and he was forced to pull up. Hansen, now desperately short of fuel, decided to take matters into his own hands and landed his aircraft. Once safely on the ground, the Bf 110s acted as mobile machine-gun positions and managed to drive off the Norwegian defenders. Enough of Wagner's Ju 52s then landed for their troops to secure the airfield. By the afternoon, the whole of the 324th Infantry Regiment had been landed along with a full military band. It was a remarkable action and Hansen's quick thinking and bravery had saved the day. As General Geisler said to Hansen when he arrived at Fornebu two days later, "but for your squadron, things might have turned out very differently."[20]

The soldiers then made their way into Oslo, and the band held an impromptu concert in the centre of the city in an effort to persuade the Norwegian population

German troops watch the Luftwaffe reduce a British position during the fighting in Norway.

that the Germans were in control. Effectively they were, as the Norwegian Government and King Haakon had already fled to Hamar. The plan had been that a special squad would capture these important figures in the early hours of the morning, but the sinking of the *Blücher* had put an end to any such possibility. Nonetheless, Captain Spiller was determined to do so. He loaded some of his paratroopers into a bus and set off for Hamar. They were met outside Oslo by a scratch force led by the new Norwegian Commander-in-Chief, General Otto Ruge (the ineffectual Laake had been replaced earlier that day). The Germans were decisively beaten, and Spiller was killed. In his pocket was found a list of people to be arrested, headed by King Haakon, the prime minister Johan Nygaardsvold, and Carl Hambro, head of the *Storting* (the Norwegian parliament).[21] Meanwhile, Vidkun Quisling had proclaimed a government of national unity and ordered the population not to resist the German invasion. Quisling's treachery merely stiffened Norwegian resistance, and the Germans soon replaced him with an Administrative Council.

It had been a stunningly successful day for the Germans. In addition to the seizure of all *Weserübung*'s objectives, Denmark had also fallen with barely a shot being fired. The only black spot had been the sinking of the *Blücher* and the failure to capture the king and government. Now it was simply a question of building up German forces and conquering the Norwegian interior. Von Falkenhorst flew in on 10 April. However, not everything was to go Germany's way. The British and French had just pledged Norway their full support, and even now the British were preparing an expeditionary force.

German mountain troops go to ground under enemy fire during a patrol north of Narvik in April 1940.

The Royal Navy, after its somewhat ineffectual performance in the build-up to *Weserübung*, began to make its presence felt. The Germans, in an effort to provide supplies for the first wave of their troops, had intended to have tankers and supply ships already in Norwegian ports. Only one tanker of the two intended for Narvik arrived, and none of the freighters. Only one of the three destined for Trondheim arrived, and that was four days late, so it was decided that most reinforcements and supplies would be channelled through Oslo, the safest and shortest route. The British submarine service had done much to disrupt this German effort. Indeed, the Polish submarine *Orzel* had sunk the transport *Rio de Janeiro* on 8 April, nearly alerting the Norwegians to the German plan. At least 10 transports or tankers were sunk in the opening days of the invasion. Captain Warborton-Lee led five destroyers into Narvikfjord and managed to sink two German destroyers, the *Heidkamp*, aboard which Commodore Bonte died, and the *Anton Schmidtt*. Warborton-Lee, however, lost his life and two British destroyers in the action. On 13 April, the battleship *Warspite* and nine destroyers entered Narvikfjord and sank the remaining seven German destroyers. General Dietl and his men were now cut off.

Naval dominance was less complete off the coast of southern and central Norway, as the German control of the air inhibited the Royal Navy's freedom of action. On the first day the destroyer HMS *Gurkha* was sunk and the battleship *Rodney* hit by Luftwaffe bombs. Yet the traffic was not all one way, as Fleet Air Arm aircraft sunk the *Königsberg* in Bergen harbour.

BRITISH TROOPS LAND IN NORWAY

On 14 April, the first British troops were landed in central and northern Norway. The British plan centred around the recapture of Trondheim. Rejecting a frontal assault down Trondheim fjord, the British chiefs of staff decided to envelop the port by landing Allied forces north and south of the city, at Namsos and Andalsnes. Meanwhile, General Ruge with what Norwegian forces he could muster hoped to contain the Germans in the passes that led out from Oslo until British support arrived in sufficient numbers. Key to this was preventing the Germans forcing their way up the Gudbrandsdal, because, should they manage to do so, the Allied attack on Trondheim would be directly threatened from the rear, and initially this plan appeared to work.

On 13 April, the day before the British landed, German troops began to push out from Oslo on three axes: east, north and west. The Germans, with powerful air support, quickly swept aside the improvised road blocks and scored some quick successes. Between 13 and 14 April, a whole regiment surrendered outside Tønsberg, southwest of Oslo, and 3000 Norwegians at Kongsvinger were forced to withdraw into Sweden to avoid encirclement. Meanwhile, German aircraft continued to bomb the improvised mobilization centres that the Norwegians had set up. Yet there were still grounds for optimism. The terrain where Ruge intended to make a stand, on a

One of Dietl's men of the 139th Gebirgsjäger Regiment, which fought bravely at Narvik in April and May 1940.

line between Randsfjord and Lake Mjøsa, was rough and might very easily delay the four German mechanized columns descending upon him.

Between 14 and 17 April, bad weather largely kept the Luftwaffe on the ground, and thus the Norwegians were able to hold on until the weather lifted on the 18th. Supported by tanks of Panzer Abteilung (Battalion) 40 – mainly Panzer Is and IIs, although a number of the short-lived NbFz PzKpfw VI heavy tanks also saw service in Norway – the Germans were able to capture Elverum and Hamar east of Lake Mjøsa, and Gjøvik and Raufoss to the west. Ruge was getting desperate. He committed his last reserves, 5000 men from the Bergen Division, and his defences were further hampered by the dropping of 200 German paratroopers behind his front. These men succeeded for a time in cutting Norwegian lines of communication before being rounded up by the Norwegians on 20 April. When he learned that the British 148th Brigade had landed at Andalsnes, Ruge demanded that rather than

attack Trondheim it should be used to consolidate the Norwegian front just south of Lillehammer. Its commander, Brigadier Morgan agreed. However, the British troops were poorly equipped and trained, and were not helped much by the hurried loading of their transport ships, which meant vital supplies and weapons were either mislaid or left behind.[22] Their first encounters with the Germans on 21 April did not go well. Two British battalions were mauled by three German battalions supported by aircraft, artillery and tanks east of Lake Mjøsa. Men from the 148th Brigade attempted to make a stand at Tretten, a key position which commanded access to the Gudbrandsdal, the following day. After finding their light anti-tank weapons ineffective against the German armour and after making a desperate defence of the town, a mere 300 men managed to retreat northwards.

The German position in Trondheim was precarious. Although the original 1700 troops had been reinforced to 4000, due to air lifts, they were very short of equipment, particularly artillery. Yet the British were not able to take advantage of this. Aware of the British landing, the Germans responded promptly and on 20 April the Luftwaffe began attacking Namsos at regular intervals. British General Carton de Wiart soon

German tanks rumble into Belgium in May 1940. The German invasion of the West forced the Allied evacuation of Norway.

found his port a shambles. He had been ordered to attack Trondheim from the north, but the move south was difficult and the roads were clogged with snow. Meanwhile, the German 181st Division under Major-General Kurt Woytasch, having secured the railway line running east to the Swedish border, turned north towards Steinkjer. Woytasch moved one infantry company north by rail, landed another by sea and managed to capture the key Verdal road bridge. These units were soon in combat with the forward companies of the King's Own Yorkshire Light Infantry. The British were pushed back, and the German landings by sea behind their forward positions further compromised their defence. De Wiart ordered his troops to retreat back to Namsos, and Steinkjer fell to the Germans on 22 April. The British were now certainly on the defensive and their strategy in central Norway was completely in tatters. De Wiart now had little military rationale for the presence of his force at Namsos, as the attack on Trondheim was now impossible. Brigadier Morgan's men were serving a vital purpose but were in danger of being outflanked as the Germans, in the face of weakening Norwegian opposition, advanced up the Østerdal Valley, which runs parallel to the Gudbrandsdal.

German troops attack at Sedan, France, in May 1940. The invasion of the West saved Dietl's men embattled at Narvik.

There was a brief respite for the Allies as French reinforcements began to arrive for de Wiart and the Germans failed to resume their advance. Carrier-based British aircraft were making an appearance over the battlefield, so morale was beginning to improve. Indeed, the French commander, General Audet, and his Norwegian counterpart, Colonel Getz, even drew up a plan to attack Steinkjer, but de Wiart, an extremely seasoned old soldier, sensing the hopelessness of the situation, turned

The Gneisenau, *seen here firing at HMS* Glorious *in June 1940, was one of the ships damaged during the invasion of Norway.*

down the offer of additional troops, as accepting them, "would have made evacuation still more difficult." Indeed the order to pull out came on 27 April.[23] To the south, General Paget had arrived with his 15th Brigade and was trying to stem the German advance in the Gudbrandsdal. His 3000 men, without vehicles, artillery, armour and air cover, faced 8500 German mechanized troops well equipped with tanks and artillery, and with complete control of the air. At Kvam, however, the 15th Brigade repulsed repeated German assaults and the Germans lost more than 50 men and 5 tanks. To quote French historian François Kersaudy, "for the first time since the British landed in Norway, this was a real battle not an execution."[24] The brigade retired in good order on the 26th, and repeated its performance at Kjørem and then at Otta. Paget had contained the German advance, but he wouldn't be able to maintain this for long without reinforcements and air cover. He requested these from the British War Office on 28 April, but was told, much to his surprise, that the British and French were evacuating central Norway. General Ruge protested, but was ignored by his allies. Nevertheless, his demoralized and exhausted troops covered the British evacuation, which was completed on 1-2 May. The remaining Norwegian forces in south and central Norway surrendered the following day.

THE BATTLE FOR NARVIK

In the north, however, the situation was somewhat different. The British had achieved complete naval dominance, being largely out of reach of German air power. They had established British, French and Polish troops ashore around the German-occupied port of Narvik. The RAF had managed to operate fighter squadrons from Bardufoss airfield and, together with the Norwegian 6th Division, the only Norwegian divisional formation to mobilize fully, the Allies prepared to assault Narvik.

Thus the situation for Dietl and his 4000 or so men – about 2000 of the 139th Gebirgsjäger Regiment and about 2500 surviving sailors from the sunken German ships – was grim. They had salvaged as many naval and anti-aircraft guns from the ships as possible, and were erratically resupplied by Ju 52 transports, which had brought in at least one battery of 75mm guns. On 9 May, two parachute companies of the 2nd Division were dropped into the Narvik area after minimal training. Dietl formed a loose defensive perimeter around the town, although he left the almost impassable terrain to the southeast guarded by a detachment of sailors. There had been some fighting, and Dietl's men had cleared the route to the Swedish border and secured the iron ore railway. The British 24th Brigade, in conjunction with the Norwegian 6th Division, had been probing his positions since 14 April. Hitler, in a panic, had suggested that Dietl and his men be airlifted out or perhaps withdrawn south, but Jodl had pointed out the impossibility of such a course.[25]

In early May, the Allies received their first tanks and landing craft. The dilatory General Mackesy finally agreed to attack the German positions around the town of Bjerkvik. On 12 May, supported by naval gunfire, French Foreign Legion troops were landed on the seafront. They came under murderous fire from the German mountain troops, but were supported by other French troops and Norwegians attacking the Germans' rear. They took the town and pushed on to the military camp at Elvegårdsmoen, which was captured after three hours of fierce hand-to-hand fighting. They next pushed on to the southern extremity of the Øyord peninsula, which would provide a useful springboard for the assault on Narvik proper.

Meanwhile, the 2nd Gebirgs Division, commanded by General Feurstein, was ordered to Trondheim, "to open up a northern overland route through which you will relieve General Dietl's forces . . . faced by superior enemy forces in the Narvik area."[26] As soon as the British had pulled out of Namsos, Feurstein started his 1200km (744-mile) march to Dietl's aid, pushing back the British and Norwegians between him and his goal. They did their best to delay him by blowing bridges and fighting short actions. On one occasion, Feurstein's men overcame a key British position by landing troops behind them by aircraft. The pace of the German advance forced the Allies to hasten their preparations for the capture of Narvik. Mackesy was replaced by General Claude Auchinleck, who did much to drive the operation forward.

Decision in France

On 10 May, the Germans put Plan *Gelb* into action and invaded France, Belgium and the Netherlands. The German success forced the British and French to reassess their commitment to Norway. On 23 May, as the situation in France worsened, the British War Cabinet discussed a chiefs of staff report, recommending that Narvik be captured prior to a total evacuation of Norway. The new British prime minister, Winston Churchill, agreed, and Auchinleck was instructed to evacuate northern Norway as quickly as possible on 25 May. He was ordered, however, to attack Narvik to cover the safe withdrawal of Allied forces and to deny future exports of iron ore to Germany by damaging Narvik's port. Covered by Royal Navy gunfire, British, French and Polish troops captured the town after bitter fighting. Despite desperate counterattacks, the Germans were being pushed back. Major Haussels was forced to order the evacuation of the town, and the French Foreign Legion began to push Dietl's men back towards the Swedish border. Hitler gave Dietl permission to retreat into Sweden and be interned if necessary. However, this did not prove necessary, as the British and French withdrew 11 days later on 8 June. King Haakon and his government left Norway on 7 June 1940. General Ruge, who preferred to stay with his men, surrendered to Dietl the following day. The campaign for Norway was over.

The British lost almost 4500 men. Some 1500 of these were aboard the aircraft carrier HMS *Glorious* and her two destroyer escorts, which were sunk by the *Scharnhorst* and *Gneisenau* during the evacuation. The French and Poles lost 500 men between them and the Norwegians about 1800. German losses were higher at about 5000. They also lost 242 aircraft, a third of them transport, in comparison to 112 from the RAF. However, it was in terms of warships that the cost of the

British anti-aircraft guns in northern Norway in May 1940. The Allies eventually captured Narvik, but only as an action to cover their evacuation from Norway.

German victory became significant. The Kriegsmarine lost 3 cruisers, 10 destroyers and 4 U-boats, while the *Scharnhorst* and *Gneisenau* sustained serious damage. By the end of the campaign, only one heavy and two light cruisers and four destroyers were fit for action. British losses were of a similar scale, but could be easily absorbed by the Royal Navy. For the far smaller German Navy, Norway was a campaign from which its surface fleet never fully recovered. It was certainly in no position to contest control of the English Channel with the Royal Navy once France was defeated.

In return for these sacrifices, Germany secured the Scandinavian minerals and iron ore route. Raeder gained the bases that he wanted so much, thus loosening British control of the Atlantic approaches and making the imposition of a British naval blockade of Germany more difficult. Once the Arctic convoys began to Russia, these bases proved particularly useful. However, Norway had to be garrisoned and proved to be a serious drain on German resources. Even the strategic importance of Norway as a naval base was lessened after the fall of France, as the French west coast ports provided the Germans with direct access to the Atlantic. This was particularly valuable to the U-boats. The campaign in Norway had demonstrated the German ability to undertake combined services operations. The Germans had proved to be far more capable than their British adversaries, although admittedly most of the British troops had been territorials. The German troops had adapted well to their environment, and as one Gebirgs soldier wrote this provided, "a foretaste of the hardships we were later to meet in Lapland."[27] The Luftwaffe had performed brilliantly, and had probably been the decisive factor, but it had lost vital transport aircraft, which had serious strategic implications for future operations.

Chapter 3

HITLER'S BARBAROSSA VENTURE

In June 1941 Hitler launched Operation Barbarossa, his invasion of the Soviet Union. In Finland Mannerheim's troops advanced relatively easily, but in the far north Dietl's men had a wretched time trying to capture Murmansk.

The Arctic campaign of the German Army is truly the story of a forgotten campaign of World War II: the Eastern Front's sector in the far north and the men who fought there, despite the inhospitable environment and climate.

Neither the Finns nor the Soviets was satisfied with the Peace of Moscow signed in March 1940. For Stalin the treaty was a poor substitute for his real ambition: the complete conquest of Finland. But at least the Soviet dictator could feel satisfied that the security of Leningrad had been immeasurably improved by the acquisition of Finnish Karelia. But Stalin did not relax his suspicious vigilance against Finland.

A German StuG III assault gun of Army Group North during the advance to Leningrad in the summer of 1941. German troops to the north of Lake Ladoga faced fighting in difficult terrain.

The Finns had even greater reason to feel dissatisfied by the treaty. Not only had they lost the great economic assets of Karelia to their worst foe, but the need to house and provide for almost half a million refugees strained Finland's war-torn economy to the limit.[1] During the Winter War Karelia had been an invaluable buffer zone that absorbed and blunted the first Soviet offensives. The new border gave the Red Army direct access to Finland's rail and road network, thus placing the heartland of the country within striking distance of another Soviet invasion. Furthermore, Finland had been forced to cede the Hanko peninsula (some 80 miles [128 km] west of Helsinki) to the USSR as well. Thus the Soviets had a base deep behind the Finnish lines within striking distance of the Finnish capital. In case of war, the Finns would be forced to detach an entire division from the eastern frontline in order to contain this Soviet bridgehead.

As if this was not enough, the general situation in the far north had also deteriorated. At Salla, the frontier had been pushed sufficiently west for the Russians to cut Finland in two (by striking from Salla towards Oulu). It was scant consolation for the Finns that the Petsamo Corridor had been returned, since the region could not be defended in winter time.[2]

In 1940 Finland was in a most unenviable position, and time was short if she was going to prepare to face a new Soviet invasion. Defence spending was increased from

A Soviet anti-tank rifle team waits patiently for a suitable target. The PTRD anti-tank rifle, with its 14.5mm cartridges, was popular as a long-range sniping weapon.

30 percent in 1939 to 40 percent of the government's budget. The Finns placed their confidence in Marshal Mannerheim, who ordered the building of new border fortifications and modernization of Finland's armed forces. By December 1940 the army as a whole had been increased to 13 infantry divisions, 2 Jäger (light infantry) brigades and 1 cavalry brigade. By Finnish standards this was a formidable force that could be raised to 16 divisions (475,000 troops).

The new Finnish Army had a lot more modern equipment than it had possessed during the Winter War. For example, it had 25 artillery battalions equipped with modern 120mm guns and 105mm howitzers. During the Winter War the Finns had had virtually no armour, but out of captured Soviet tanks and re-equipped six-ton Vickers-Armstrong tanks they formed the 1st Tank Battalion, and with light Soviet T-37/T-38 tanks formed seven independent tank platoons as support for the infantry (tanks in fact were to play only a minor role in the Arctic war).

The Finnish Air Force was also re-equipped. By 1941 it had 152 modern aircraft, including 43 US Brewsters (B 239s), 9 British Hawker Hurricanes and 29 Bristol Blenheims.[3]

A Soviet artillery crew takes careful aim during the early weeks of Barbarossa. The gun is a 76mm F-22 field gun, which was in widespread use throughout the Red Army.

In June 1940 the Red Army invaded and occupied the hapless Baltic States (Estonia, Latvia and Lithuania), and a few weeks later Stalin forced the Romanians to cede the provinces of northern Bukovina and Bessarabia.[4] Finland had been duly warned, and as if to reinforce the Soviet threat Molotov warned the Finnish ambassador, Juhani Paasakivi, that the Petsamo nickel mines had to be controlled by a Soviet-Finnish company. When Paasakivi prevaricated Molotov exploded: "We are not interested in the ore, but in the area itself. The British must be cleared out."[5]

The terrain on the Arctic Front presented a huge problem in moving equipment. Here, a Russian gun crew manhandles its weapon (a 76mm ZiS-3) and limber across a small stream.

(The mines were owned and operated by a Anglo-Canadian company.) Obviously, Stalin was only looking for an excuse to settle scores with Finland.

The Finns looked to Sweden for assistance but the Swedes were too afraid of Moscow's displeasure.[6] That left Finland with one other ally: Germany. But Hitler was allied with Stalin, had supported the latter during the Winter War, and most Finns (including Mannerheim) found the Nazi ideology as objectionable as Soviet communism. But Finland had few choices, and in August 1940 Lieutenant-Colonel

Veltjens – Hitler's personal emissary – arrived in Helsinki on a most delicate mission. Veltjens wanted the Finns to allow the Germans to use their railways to transport troops and supplies to northern Norway. The Finns readily agreed, and on 12 September a transit agreement was signed. The Germans were allowed to set up their own communications bases at Vaasa, Rovaniemi and Ivalo, manned by 1100 administrative staff. In return the Germans would deliver 300 artillery guns, 500 anti-tank guns, 650,000 grenades and 50 modern fighter aircraft. A week later the first German troops landed in Vaasa.

The Finns viewed these developments as positive, as a way of keeping Stalin at bay. But why did Hitler change his mind about Finland? First, Hitler needed Finnish nickel as much as he needed Romania's oil. German stocks were running dangerous low and the only source of this crucial ore was to be found at Kolosjoki. In June 1940, the Finns and Germans made an agreement that secured 70 percent of the mine's output for Germany. When Molotov visited Berlin in November 1940, Hitler and the obdurate Soviet foreign minister had a violent fallout concerning Finland and its nickel ore. Hitler forbade any Soviet threats against Finland that could jeopardize the flow of supplies to Germany.[7] Hitler had been planning to invade the USSR since the summer of 1940, and the meeting with Molotov only confirmed his decision to deal with Stalin once and for all. Perhaps Finland could play a role in securing the northern flank of Operation Barbarossa, the codename for the invasion of the USSR, and help divert Soviet troops to a secondary front.

Initial plans to invade the USSR drawn up by the OKW in early August 1940 did not envisage any role

for Finland. That all changed a few weeks later when the plans were redrawn. The Finns could now cut the 1400km- (875-mile-) long Murmansk railway, the Germans could occupy Petsamo, and finally the Finnish Army could assist in the blockade of Leningrad by occupying Karelia and linking up with the German Army Group North at Tikhvin.

On 5 December 1940, the Germans stated that they expected the Finns to cooperate with these plans, and informed them that two German mountain divisions would be deployed in the Arctic. Two days later, the German planners wanted to use four divisions in the far north. Even more ambitious were plans that Colonel Buschenhagen, the Chief of Staff of the German Army of Norway, had drawn up in collaboration with General Franz Halder. These plans proposed a simultaneous offensive against Salla and Murmansk.

On 18 December 1940, Hitler approved Directive 21 which outlined the planned invasion of the USSR. Finland's role was to "neutralize" the Soviet Hanko base and cooperate closely with Army Group North's drive on Leningrad by attacking on both sides of Lake Ladoga. "Force North" was to occupy Petsamo in the clumsily named Operation Reindeer. Hitler's morbid fears about the security in Norway were such that Force North was not to attack the Murmansk sector. In any case, as the envisaged invasion was to defeat the USSR in a mere two to four months, it was felt that a large-scale operation against Murmansk was an unnecessary diversion of effort. For reasons of security the Finns were not told of the German plans, and when the

A Finnish patrol west of Salla in early 1941. As part of the Barbarossa plan, Finnish and German troops attacked east into Soviet Karelia.

Finnish General Talvela came to Berlin for talks he was simply asked if the Finns could mobilize "inconspicuously".[8]

At the end of December 1940 General Nikolaus von Falkenhorst, the commander of the German Army of Norway, was instructed by the OKW to draw up new and more detailed plans for operations in the Arctic. By 27 January 1941, Buschenhagen had completed his plan codenamed Operation Silverfox (*Silberfuchs*). Petsamo was still to be occupied, but farther south the Finnish III Corps was to make a thrust towards Kem via Ukhta. The German force – XXXVI Corps – was to cut off the Kola peninsula by making a thrust via Salla and occupy Kandalaksha, thus cutting the Murmansk railway and isolating Murmansk. Once that had been accomplished, XXXVI Corps was to swing north and, as the Petsamo force moved on the port from the west, would attack Murmansk from the south. The Finns were to make their main contribution in the south by concentrating their forces in an offensive towards the River Svir north of Lake Ladoga, and holding the frontline from Ladoga to Salla with weak forces. The Finns were still kept in the dark, though, despite the fact that their participation was crucial for the success of Silverfox.[9]

On 3 February Hitler approved Operation Barbarossa. According to this final plan, Silverfox was only to be launched once Finland was involved in a war with Russia. The Oberkommando der Wehrmacht (OKW) – German Armed Forces

German armoured personnel carrier, trucks and light vehicles near Leningrad in the autumn of 1941. By this date the Finns had also made good progress towards the Soviet city.

High Command – believed operational possibilities in the Arctic were poor and that no strong force could operate from Petsamo on its own. Everything hinged upon Sweden allowing troops to be transferred from Norway to Finland on its railways and the Finns offering full cooperation. At the end of February Buschenhagen flew to Helsinki for talks with the Finnish general staff. The Finns appreciated the German offer of defending the Arctic north and Lapland, but their strategic aims were limited to liberating Soviet-occupied Karelia. They would not attack the USSR without a good cause or provocation from Stalin. Thus the Arctic operations were to be crippled by the lack of common aims and planning between the Axis allies. Hitler drove yet another nail in the coffin for the success of Silverfox when he, after the British raids on the Lofoten Islands in March, refused to transfer 40 percent of the Army of Norway's strength to the Arctic Front. At least von Falkenhorst had been relieved of overall control, since all the Arctic and Finnish operations were placed under OKW supervision.[10]

"THE REGION IS UNSUITED TO MILITARY OPERATIONS"

During the latter part of 1940, the German 2nd Mountain Division had been transported along the coast and assembled at the small "town" of Alta. The designated commander of Mountain Corps Norway was the victor of Narvik: General Eduard Dietl. Dietl placed his troops camped around the Varangerfjord, and here they were left to hibernate during the winter of 1940–41. Dietl saw this region as a miserable "desert" of a place both during summers and winters. He concluded: "There has never been a war fought in the high north . . . The region is unsuited to military operations. There are no roads and these would have to be constructed before any advance could take place."[11] Without good roads, lacking heavy equipment and faced with enormous logistical and natural obstacles, an offensive against Murmansk was doomed from the start.[12] But when General Feurstein, the commander of the 2nd Mountain Division, made a whole series of objections to taking the offensive, Dietl replied that he was aware of these but they would have to be overcome at all cost. He had Feurstein replaced by General Schlemmer on 28 March 1941.

Afterwards Dietl flew to Berlin and attended the Führer conference in the Reich Chancellery in Berlin, where Hitler was to brief his generals before Barbarossa. Having attended to the main front, Hitler turned to a large wall map and pointed at Murmansk. This was the USSR's only all-year-round ice-free port that could be used in combination with the strategic Murmansk railway to supply the USSR with war materiel from Britain and the USA. It could, furthermore, be used by the Soviet Fourteenth Army to threaten Petsamo and the all-important nickel mines. Confident of Finnish support, Hitler wanted Dietl to secure the mines and occupy Murmansk. Hitler called the distance from the Finnish border to Murmansk – only 120km (74 miles) – "laughable", and seemed to expect his favourite general to undertake the operation like a summer promenade. Dietl,

Waffen-SS troops fighting in Russia during Operation Barbarossa. They may have performed well south of Leningrad, but in the far north SS troops earned nothing but derision.

who actually knew the region, pointed out that the Kola and Murmansk region looked like the world on its first day of creation: all bare rocks, huge boulders, rushing waters and no trees or vegetation. During the winter it was transformed into an icy hell on earth, with temperatures plunging as low as minus 50 degrees Celsius. The short summers were no better. There were continuous rains which turned the thawed ground into a huge swamp – as the permafrost did not allow rain to seep deep into the ground – filled with clouds of mosquitoes. Dietl pointed out that the Finns chose to abandon all the territory north of the 65th Parallel during the winter, thus leaving the 800km (500 miles) from Suomassalmi to Petsamo unguarded except for a few patrols on skis.

Dietl suggested instead that he only occupy Petsamo, and make a single strike against Kandalaksha to cut the Murmansk railway. Thus Murmansk would be isolated from rest of Russia and rendered useless as a port. Then, if the circumstances allowed, the Germans could proceed to attack Murmansk. Hitler seemed to listen to Dietl's objections to begin with, but then drew his own fatal and idiosyncratic conclusions. The German Lapland Army was to be split three ways: Dietl was still to march on Murmansk, XXXVI Corps was to attack Salla and capture Kandalaksha, some 200km (125 miles) south of Dietl, and finally III Corps was to cut the Murmansk railway at Louhi – yet another 350km (219 miles) farther south. Thus in addition to keeping the troops needed for the Arctic in Norway, Hitler now ensured failure by unnecessarily dispersing the forces which were available.[13]

Buschenhagen's visit to Helsinki had alerted the Finns to German plans but they did not know any of the details and what role, if any, they were to play in Hitler's grand scheme of things. Privately, President Ryti was convinced that Hitler, having failed to invade Great Britain, would now turn his attentions towards Stalin, and he

Finnish infantry advance under cover of a smoke-screen during Mannerheim's advance to Lake Ladoga in June 1941.

A Soviet soldier surrenders to Finnish troops during the advance towards Leningrad. In general, the Red Army conducted a competent retreat in the face of the Finnish Army.

handed over the responsibility for military talks with the Germans to Mannerheim. The marshal picked his right-hand man and chief of staff, Lieutenant-General Erik Heinrichs, to head these talks.

Heinrichs went to Salzburg on 25 May 1941 where General Alfred Jodl briefed him about the German plans. Jodl wanted the Finns to tie up the Soviet forces north of Lake Ladoga, assist III Corps at Salla, and patrol with light troops the area from Salla to Petsamo to cover the gap in the German lines. He also wanted to use Finnish airfields and facilities. Heinrichs was non-committal. He believed the Germans had arrogantly underestimated the Red Army (whom Heinrichs had experience in fighting and the Germans had not), and the natural obstacles to an Arctic war. He believed the Germans would not succeed because the Russians would prove formidable foes in defence of their Motherland. Heinrichs was also worried that the German attack could trigger a pre-emptive Soviet strike against Finland.

On 26 May Heinrichs flew on to Berlin and talked to Halder, who was even more forthcoming and ambitious on behalf of Germany's new self-imposed ally. He wanted the Finns to strike against the Karelian Isthmus and Leningrad. Heinrichs, however, a diplomatic and cool character, would not be drawn into any commitments on behalf of his country.[14]

Heinrichs' superiors in Helsinki did not share the general's caution nor his wish for Finland to remain neutral. Ryti hoped that Germany would win a war against the USSR, but hoped Finland should and could stay out. For his part, Mannerheim was willing to take risks and believed this was a golden opportunity to settle scores with the USSR.

Despite Finnish hesitation the Germans went ahead with their plans. Silverfox, including Reindeer, was to be carried out by Dietl's Mountain Corps Norway (2nd and 3rd Mountain – Gebirgs – Divisions), but the occupation of Murmansk would depend upon occupying the Soviet Northern Fleet's base of Polyarny. Farther south, XXXVI Corps, ordered to carry out Operation Polarfox against Kandalaksha, was being concentrated around Rovaniemi. Everything was now prepared for the invasion of the USSR.

On 22 June 1941, Operation Barbarossa was launched against the USSR with 3 million troops, 3500 tanks and 2000 aircraft on a front that stretched from the Black Sea to the Baltic.[15] It was a huge gamble since Hitler had staked everything on one giant card: to knock out Stalin's empire with a single, massive military blow before the winter set in. Having concluded the war in the East, Hitler would turn his attentions against Great Britain once again.

THE FINNS JOIN BARBAROSSA

In Finland all was quiet. But it was the calm before the storm. Given Germany's preparations in and around the country it was inevitable that Finland would, whether it liked it or not, be dragged into the war on Hitler's side. On the morning of 22 June Hitler's proclamation read: "Together with their Finnish comrades in arms the heroes from Narvik stand at the edge of the Arctic Ocean. German troops under command of the conqueror of Norway and the Finnish freedom fighters under their Marshal's command are protecting Finnish territory." Stalin was naturally convinced that Finland had joined Hitler, and so three days later Soviet bombers attacked targets in southern Finland. On 26 June Finnish border troops were placed on alert.

The Finns had already commenced their operations days earlier. On 19 June Major-General Airo (Quartermaster General of the Finnish Army) was put in charge of Operation Regatta: the occupation of the "demilitarized" Aland archipelago. During the night of 21/22 June, some 5200 troops with 69 artillery guns were transported, while being strafed by Soviet aircraft, across the waters to Aland. All the approaches to Aland were blocked by the Finnish Navy in cooperation with the Swedish Navy.[16]

This raised the question of Sweden's role in the Arctic war and how far it would cooperate with Germany and Finland. The Swedish Government – a coalition government headed and dominated by the socialists – was adamantly opposed to any

The far northern arm of Barbarossa. The advance started well enough, but then the Finns halted and dug in north of Leningrad, while Dietl's drive on Murmansk ran into fierce resistance and petered out.

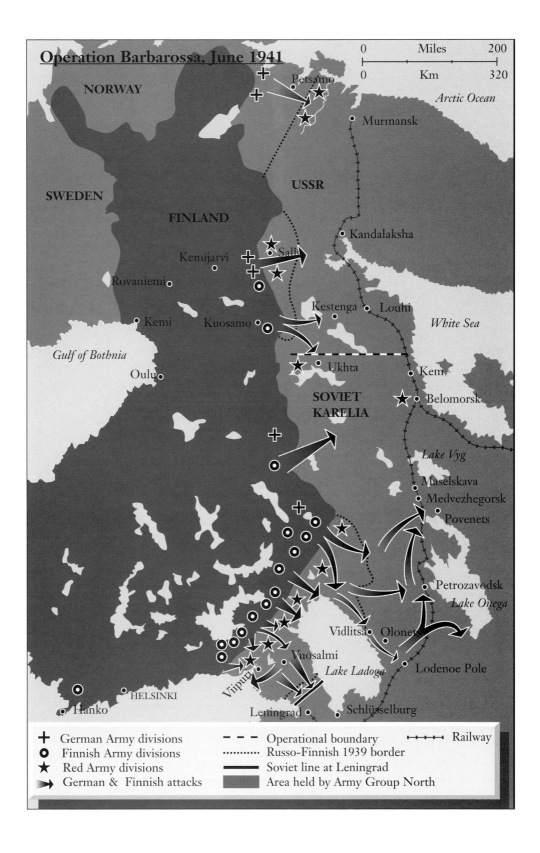

Operation Barbarossa, June 1941

| 0 | Miles | 200 |
| 0 | Km | 320 |

NORWAY

Petsamo

Arctic Ocean

Murmansk

SWEDEN

USSR

FINLAND

Kandalaksha

Kemijarvi

Salla

Rovaniemi

Kestenga   Louhi

Kemi   Kuosamo

White Sea

Gulf of Bothnia

Ukhta   Kem

Oulu

SOVIET
KARELIA

Belomorsk

Lake Vyg

Maselskava

Medvezhegorsk

Povenets

Petrozavodsk
Lake Onega

Vidlitsa   Olonets

Vuosalmi

Lake Ladoga

Lodenoe Pole

Viipuri

HELSINKI

Hanko

Leningrad   Schlüsselburg

+	German Army divisions	– – –	Operational boundary	+++++	Railway
⊙	Finnish Army divisions	··········	Russo-Finnish 1939 border		
★	Red Army divisions	——	Soviet line at Leningrad		
➤	German & Finnish attacks		Area held by Army Group North		

idea of an alliance with Hitler but were willing to grant Germany major concessions. They dropped restrictions on the number of German troops that could cross Swedish territory and, typical of Sweden's often unprincipled and short-sighted foreign policy, gave in to the German demand that the 163rd (Engelbrecht) Infantry Division (of 14,712 troops) be allowed to cross Sweden with all its arms and equipment.[17] Colonel Helmer Bratt, the commandant of Boden Fortress in northern Sweden, gave orders that the fortresses' guns were to be ranged at all times against the town's rail station while the Germans were present there. The division's commander, Lieutenant-General Erwin Engelbrechten, protested at Swedish hostility when he was confronted by fully armed Swedish troops at the station.[18] No wonder that Hitler claimed: "We can expect nothing from Sweden."[19]

But could he expect more from his erstwhile ally Finland? The Finns made it quite clear that there was no political alliance between themselves and Hitler's Germany. Finland was conducting, they claimed, a separate and different war from that of Germany. Mannerheim planned simply to take the territory lost in 1940, and then advance up to an easily defended triangle of Karelian territory bounded by Lakes Onega, Ladoga, Segozero and the Svir River. The plan was for the Germans and Finns to link up at the Svir and thus cut off Leningrad completely from the rest of the Soviet Union. Ladoga split the Finnish front in two, and the Finnish Army had only enough strength to launch one offensive at the time. Mannerheim would begin with Karelia.

THE ORDERS OF BATTLE

By 29 June the Finnish Army had completed its concentration along the border. It was made up of five army corps (including III Corps under indirect German command) with 13 divisions, some two divisions (headquarters reserve) and one division (the 17th) blocking the Soviet Hanko base. What about the Soviet forces? Those facing Finland were under the command of Marshal Voroshilov and the Leningrad Military District. The Twenty-Third Army (General Gerasimov), of four divisions, covered Leningrad from the north across the Karelian Isthmus, with the Seventh (General Meretskov) covering the frontier from Ladoga to Ukhta, with three divisions along the frontier and two in reserve. And in the north stood the Fourteenth Army with four divisions, including one armoured division (as reserve), covering the frontier from Ukhta to the Arctic coast. The Hanko garrison consisted of 27–30,000 troops. The Finns (with 230,000 men) faced 150,000 Russians north of Lake Ladoga and on the Isthmus. A not inconsiderable numerical superiority, it would be needed as the Soviets had been able to prepare their defences since the beginning of Barbarossa.

On 26 June Mannerheim had appointed Heinrichs as commander of the Karelian Army with five divisions and 100,000 troops. The Finnish offensive began on 10 July, and six days later the Finns reached Lake Ladoga. Thus the Soviet armies were cut off

German troops in a trench during the investment of Leningrad in late 1941. Finnish efforts to capture the city were half-hearted to say the least.

from each other. The Karelian Army's drive along the Ladoga route encountered stiff resistance from Colonel Bondarev's Soviet 168th Division. By 7 August that unit, as well as another division, was trapped against the coast and three days later three Finnish divisions moved in for the kill. But Bondarev organized a splendid fighting retreat and created a well-defended bridgehead, from where the Soviet Ladoga Flotilla evacuated the two divisions to the Russian-held shore. Farther north the Engelbrecht Division's advance (from Joensuu) was slowed down by the Russians using the new T-34 tanks. By 9 September the troops had reached Mannerheim's first stop line.

This allowed the marshal to turn to his second stage of the campaign: the conquest of the Karelian Isthmus. II Corps was to clear the northern bank of the Vuoksi River and outflank Viipuri. Then IV Corps was to attack Viipuri and trap any Russian forces there. The offensive opened on 31 July but made slow progress, forcing Mannerheim to call in the 3rd Division as well. The Soviet 198th and 142nd Divisions were trapped against Lake Ladoga, but due to brilliant Russian rearguard action they were evacuated by the Ladoga Flotilla. Nevertheless, the Finns had cleared the entire northern bank by 23 August.

The Finns crossed the Vuoksi and trapped another three divisions around Viipuri, which was cut off from Leningrad by 27 August. Instead of crushing this pocket, Mannerheim, for political rather than strategic reasons, sent his army racing to the old border. On 29 August the Russians counterattacked and gained a wide enough gap in the Finnish line for two of their divisions to escape. The third Soviet division, holed up on Koivisto Island outside Viipuri, was evacuated to Leningrad. Yet by 9 September the Finns had achieved their strategic aim: holding all territory up to the old border. The day before, the Germans had cut off Leningrad's communications with the rest of the USSR by capturing Schlüsselburg. The Germans had already requested Finnish assistance in capturing the proud Russian city, but Mannerheim answered (on 27 August) that Finland had no interest in that objective and lacked the heavy artillery and dive-bombers necessary for a long siege of a well-fortified city.

Meanwhile the Karelian Army, now rested and facing the Soviet Seventh Army, divided into two corps (of two divisions each), launched a new offensive on 3 September. The offensive was spearheaded by Colonel Lagus' motorized force. Olonets was captured on the 6th, the Svir reached the day after and, on 8 September, a major strategic success was achieved: the Finns captured Lodenoe Pole and had therefore cut the Murmansk railway.

On 2 September the Finn's left flank had begun the offensive towards Petrozavodsk – the capital of Soviet Karelia situated on the western shore of Lake Onega. The Finns avoided a costly frontal assault and instead outmanoeuvred the Russians by making flank attacks through the wilderness. Russian morale, however, remained high. During a five-week period the Soviet 3rd Division broke out of several Finnish traps set for it, and managed to reach the final Soviet frontline safely. By early October the entire course of the Svir River was cleared of Soviet troops, but the Finnish

A soldier of the Waffen-SS Totenkopf *Division, which was recruited from concentration camp guards. Soldiers from this division served with the 6th SS Mountain Division in Finland in 1941.*

A Finnish Brewster takes to the air during an operation in 1941. The Finnish Air Force was small, but gave valuable service throughout the war.

offensive was running out of steam. The troops were in fact becoming more mutinous the farther east they moved.

To secure the Karelian Army's northern flank, Heinrichs made a premature offensive against Maselskaya and Medvezhegorsk. Poor preparations, the troops' low morale and battle fatigue, coupled with stiffening Soviet resistance, meant that the offensive failed. To secure the newly built spur line of the Murmansk railway line (from Belomorsk to Archangel) the Soviet Stavka (General Headquarters) had placed two divisions around Belomorsk. The Finns also encountered the élite 114th Division made up of redoubtable Siberians, who were as tough as the Finns themselves. Between 7 and 21 November, the Finnish offensive stalled as even the élite Jäger battalion refused to attack.

A new offensive was launched on 5 December in minus 30 degrees Celsius of frost and blinding snow. The day after, Medvezhegorsk was captured and two Soviet divisions were deliberately sacrificed to delay the Finnish advance. Having destroyed the last pockets of Soviet resistance, the Finnish Army went on the defensive on 12 December. Few Finns realized or would have suspected that their army would remain on the defensive for another three years. The campaign had cost the Finns 25,000 dead and 50,000 wounded – a heavy toll for a nation of barely three million that had already lost many casualties during the Winter War.

The concentration of Dietl's Mountain Corps Norway was a massive undertaking in itself, not only because of the distances involved but also because of the precarious lines of communication to Finnmark (the northern part of Norway), where his corps was to be concentrated. In Norway and Finland the railway reached only as far north as Narvik and Rovaniemi respectively, and the capacity of the Oulu to Rovaniemi line was quite limited. As for the roads, these were in no better shape. The Arctic Highway from Rovaniemi via Ivalo to Petsamo was a narrow dirt road often blocked during winter by heavy snowstorms. Route (*Reichsstrasse*) 50 was equally narrow and had a limited load capacity. In June 1941 it was blocked by thaw and quite impassable. The long and precarious sea route along Norway's inhospitable coastline was exposed to Russian submarine and Allied naval attacks. The ports of southern Finland, although safe, had poor capacity and were blocked by ice for up to five months during the winter.

A Soviet infantry squad moves from the dense forest into a clearing. The men are all armed with submachine guns, which were physically easier to manipulate than rifles in the close confines of wooded areas.

Nevertheless, the 2nd and 3rd Mountain Divisions, a total of 27,500 men, were in place in and around Kirkenes by late June.[20] During the night of 21/22 June Dietl's corps crossed the Finnish border (the Pasvik and Jakobs Rivers) into the Petsamo Corridor. Its first objective was to occupy Parkkina, a small town which housed various foreign consulates. His force spread out to build new roads and improve old ones while it waited for new orders. At least Dietl had completed Operation Reindeer, but what about Silverfox: the march on Murmansk?[21] Finland had still not entered the war, and had no wish to provoke Russia and Stalin by allowing the Germans to use the Corridor as a staging area for the invasion of the Soviet Murmansk region. By not entering the fray, Finland had crippled Dietl's chances of success since he had lost the vital element of surprise, which explained much of the Wehrmacht's success on the main front farther south.

It was not until a week later, therefore, that Dietl's corps could finally begin Silverfox. At 03:00 hours on the morning of 29 June, the Jägers crossed the Soviet frontier. It was immediately obvious that their superiors back in Germany and at the headquarters in Rovaniemi had completely underestimated the problems on this front. Lacking up-to-date maps, German cartographers had allowed their imagination to run riot in an effort to fill out the blank spaces on the maps they did have. What they thought were roads on the Russian maps turned out to be telegraph lines and the route of the actual Soviet-Finnish border! Such lapses in accurate or even minimal intelligence about this extremely remote region of the USSR was to cripple Dietl's chances from the beginning.

A SLOW ADVANCE

The 2nd Mountain Division had orders to make a breach in the strong line of fortifications along the Soviet border, and it had heavy artillery to support its efforts: the superb 88mm guns. German pioneers blew holes in the barbed wire. By 09.00 hours the high ground had been captured, and the Jägers had to use flamethrowers, hand grenades and explosive charges to reduce the heavy Soviet concrete bunkers one by one. The 88mm guns were also put to good use against stubborn resistance from the mainly Soviet Asiatic troops that manned them. These tough soldiers preferred a fight to the death rather than ignominious surrender.

But the Germans were not simply going to batter their way through the Soviet defences using brute force. Colonel Hengl, commander of the 137th Regiment, had been ordered to take his unit south in order to outflank the Soviet fortified line. Just as the Germans were set to advance, a heavy fogbank rolled in from the Arctic Ocean and the planned Stuka attack had to be cancelled. Instead, the 137th was forced to advance slowly and cautiously through the impenetrable fog. By 04.30 hours the fog had lifted and the advancing line of Jägers was revealed to the Soviet defenders, who opened up a deadly and withering fire against the Germans. Led by Hengl, the Jägers coolly stormed Height 204 and then descended into the Titovka Valley and secured a bridge to cross the river. They managed, despite Russian resistance, to establish a bridgehead on the river's eastern bank. By the following morning Hengl could report to Dietl that the Soviet line was broken, the enemy was retreating and could be pursued from the bridgehead.

Farther north along the Arctic coastline things were not going as smoothly for the Germans. General Schlemmer, commander of the 2nd Mountain Division, had ordered Colonel Hake's 136th Regiment to block the neck across the Rybachiy Poluostrov (the Fishermen's Peninsula). This was to prevent the peninsula being used a base for Russian counterattacks. Hake had completely underestimated the task at hand and detached only two battalions to capture the neck. A single battalion was to hold the position afterwards. Despite the ground being strewn with boulders, covered partly in snow and dominated by bogs, the 136th covered the distance from the starting line to the neck in a mere six hours.[22] So far so good. But on this front the Germans were not only denied the benefits of surprise but faced an equally strong enemy in the air – and one who was also putting his naval supremacy to good use. The Soviet Northern Fleet, stationed at Polyarny, was not one of the strongest fleets in Stalin's navy but was to prove a worthy and energetic opponent. The sailors and marines from the fleet were to prove a formidable force for the Jägers to reckon with, and worthy of their macabre nickname: "striped death" (from their blue and white striped sailor's shirts). Other defending forces of the vital Murmansk region included the Fourteenth Army consisting of two divisions, the 14th and 52nd, as well as several other smaller units of handpicked and élite troops. The peninsula itself was held by one infantry regiment supported by both field and heavy artillery.[23]

SILVERFOX STALLS

Within hours of the Germans reaching the neck of the peninsula, the Russians counterattacked while two transport ships, escorted by two Soviet destroyers, landed marines at Kutovaya near the neck. Hard-pressed from two directions, it took even the disciplined and tough Jägers over five hours to beat back and defeat their attackers. It was obvious that it would require the entire regiment to hold the neck, and it was only by using his very last reserves that Hake managed to fill the gaps in his line.[24]

The Germans had achieved their initial breakthrough and the Mountain Corps advanced farther east until it reached the Litsa River, which was blocked by two Soviet regiments. The defenders were better prepared than on the Titovka River, and the Germans managed only to get a single battalion across to the east bank, where they established a 1.6km- (1-mile-) wide bridgehead. On 7 July the Russians counterattacked, and Dietl was forced to request additional reinforcements. He would get a single motorized machine-gun battalion from Norway.

Dietl had had his forebodings about Silverfox from the start and these fears were now being realized. The lack of roads slowed down his advance and made it impos-

Troops of the German 6th SS Mountain Division in Finland. Comprised of elderly, untrained soldiers, it suffered high casualties against the Red Army.

sible to use proper motorized modes of transport. He was forced to rely on pack mules, which only brought in a trickle of supplies, while his troops were faced by terrain that made even the easiest and shortest distances a battle of willpower in the face of a determined and resourceful enemy. He could not emulate the Blitzkrieg being fought farther south and he had to improvise. Hitler, impatient as ever, pressed and pestered von Falkenhorst to get the advance going as soon as possible. But Dietl had to repeat, again and again, the impossibility of fighting a Blitzkrieg in the far north.

On 10 July a German despatch rider carrying the German offensive plans drove too far and fell into Russian hands. A whole new plan had to be drawn up. The 2nd

Division was to break out of the bridgehead and drive 6 miles (9.6km) to the south-east. Meanwhile, the 3rd Division was to establish another bridgehead farther south along the river. On 13 July the 2nd Division attacked and made good progress: some 2 miles (3.2km) eastwards. But the day after the Soviets landed two battalions on either side of Litsa Bay, which forced Dietl to break off the attack and divert troops from the bridgehead to the neck of the peninsula. His thinly stretched forces were hard pressed to hold a 57km (36-mile) frontline that extended from the Litsa to the neck. Dietl argued during four days (21–24 July) for reinforcements but Hitler, ever fearful about British attacks on Norway, refused to send any to him. Hitler's fears were not groundless, since carrier-based British aircraft bombed Petsamo and Liinahamari during the last week of July. But he agreed, nevertheless, on 30 July to transfer the 6th Mountain Division to Dietl's command.

Dietl did not give up, and during attacks by the 2nd Division (during 2–5 August) he managed to defeat two Russian battalions. Hitler then relented, and on 12 August agreed to transfer two infantry regiments (388th and 9th SS) from Norway to

Red Army T-26 tanks and ski-borne infantry launch an attack on the Finnish Front in late 1941.

Fresh from the bakery, direct to your bunker! Loaves of bread are being loaded onto sledges for transportation to the front line. Russian horses were known for their hardiness and ability to survive in the most extreme environments.

Mountain Corps Norway. This encouraged Dietl to make new plans for an offensive in September before the onset of winter made it impossible to fight. The plan was for the 2nd Mountain Division to use the 9th SS Regiment to spearhead an offensive southwards to a junction between the two main roads leading to Murmansk. Meanwhile, the 388th Regiment was to make a frontal assault upon the Soviet lines. The offensive was planned to begin on 8 September.

On 30 August, however, Russian submarines sank two German transport ships, which would delay the arrival of the 6th Mountain Division until October. On 7 September, British surface ships attacked a German convoy at the North Cape. Dietl's precarious supply line from the south was under threat, and could spell the end of his plans should the Anglo-Russian naval forces be able to interrupt German shipping completely.

On the morning of 8 September Dietl's divisions launched their attack as planned. The frontal assault by the 388th failed completely. The troops duly crossed the Titovka and stormed the hills opposite, but once the German artillery barrage lifted, bypassed Russian units opened a devastating fire upon the advancing Germans. By early afternoon 60 percent of the regiment were casualties, and a belated permission was given for the unit to withdraw before it was completely destroyed. Its counterpart, the 9th SS, was just as unlucky. The SS troops advanced on Hill 173 but they

were shot to pieces by savage Russian fire. The unit, made up of untrained and unseasoned troops no better than armed police, broke and fled for their lives (regular army prejudices about the Waffen-SS were to be amply justified on this front, as they were farther south on the Salla Front). Nevertheless, by 9 September the Jägers had reached within 480m (300yd) of the road junction when they were halted by Soviet bunkers and barbed-wire defences. The following day Soviet counterattacks stopped the German advance completely, and von Falkenhorst (pressed by an exasperated Hitler) asked Dietl tersely what was holding up the advance. Dietl was not amused at his superior's rebuke, and told von Falkenhorst in no uncertain terms that the enemy's resistance and a whole host of other problems not foreseen was holding him up.

The situation at the front was not helped by further bad news. During the summer of 1941 the British sent a small battle fleet of two aircraft carriers, two cruisers and six destroyers to the Barents Sea to support their new ally by disrupting German sea communications. But the 11 Soviet submarines placed by the Russian Northern Fleet along the north Norwegian coastline proved a much more deadly threat to

The M1910 Maxim gun was mounted on a Sokolov two-wheeled chassis. The shield provided some protection for the two-man crew. Like the majority of Soviet weaponry, it was simply constructed and easy to maintain.

German shipping than the British surface ships. On 13 September, it was reported that the Mountain Corps had only another 18 days of fuel in stock and that the troops' rations would only last until the end of September. That same day, another two transport ships were sunk and von Falkenhorst prohibited German shipping from sailing east of the North Cape.

On 17 September, German intelligence had identified a third Soviet division – the Polyarny Division (made up of sailors, convicts and volunteers) – in the sector and the day after this same division attacked the Litsa bridgehead. On 21 September the German offensive was broken off. By mid-October, the 2nd Mountain Division had withdrawn for a well-deserved rest around Petsamo, while the 6th Mountain Division, having arrived, replaced the 3rd along the Litsa Front.

The Arctic offensive had come to a halt and it would never be revived, despite plans for a new offensive during the spring of 1942. During a two-and-a-half-month offensive, Mountain Corps Norway had advanced a mere 24km (15 miles) at the phenomenal cost of 10,300 casualties. In other words, between a third and half of Dietl's troops had become casualties, which was an unprecedented level of loss for such a small force. It offered final proof of how arduous and savage the fighting was on this frontline at the "end of the world".[25]

OPERATION POLARFOX

In addition to Dietl's Arctic offensive, Hitler had also in his "wisdom" decided that yet another offensive farther south was to be staged by a second German corps – XXXVI – commanded by General der Kavallerie Feige. Feige was also in command (theoretically) of a Finnish force – III Corps – led by Finnish General Herman Siilasvuo, one of the toughest and most experienced Winter War generals Finland had. Siilasvuo, his officers and men were all veteran Arctic fighters.[26] Feige's headquarters staff (some 10,600 troops) were shipped from Oslo to Kirkenes, while the 169th Division was shipped directly from Stettin to Oulu and then on to Rovaniemi by train. These movements were codenamed "Bluefox 1" and "2".

The final unit, SS-Infantry Kampfgruppe *Nord* (Fighting Group North) was to be dogged by misfortune, and it was not an auspicious start to its campaign when its transport ship, M/S *Blenheim*, caught fire. Some 110 troops were killed. The unit was renamed (inappropriately) as the 6th SS Mountain Division.[27] It was made up of the 6th and 7th Motorized SS Infantry Regiments, two artillery battalions and one reconnaissance battalion. In total 8000 untrained, inexperienced troops and all of them in their thirties. Not only were they not suitable for Arctic forest fighting, but they were really a police formation and not combat troops. They were most certainly not cut out to take on the responsibility of an entire division on the frontline.

On 17 July 1941 SS-Gruppenführer (Lieutenant-General) Demelhuber was appointed commander of this dubious unit. He was not pleased with what he saw, but believed he could lick the men into shape if he was given three months to train them. He was given three days to get his men from Rovaniemi to the frontier along a single dirt road reserved for vehicle traffic, which forced his exhausted men to make their way through the forests surrounding the road as best they could.

The front they were up against was one of the worst in the entire theatre. South of Salla town lay the Salla Heights of 610m (2000ft), which dominated the approaches from the west and gave the Russians a clear field of observation all the way to the frontier, some 4.8km (3 miles) away. The area was held by the Soviet 122nd Rifle (i.e. Infantry) Division and 50 tanks.

The ultimate aim of Feige's force was to take Salla, move along the railway eastwards and capture Kandalaksha and thus cut the Murmansk line. The Finnish 6th Division stationed at Kuusamo, 72km (45 miles) south of Salla, was to attack northwards and capture Allakurtti and Kayrala. North of Salla the 169th Division was to attack with each of its three regiments against the Tennio River, north of Salla, and frontally against the Soviet border defences. The 6th SS Mountain Division was to send its two regiments along the Salla-Kandalaksha road from the south. General Siilasvou's ultimate aim was to cut the Murmansk line at Loukhi and Kem with the Finnish 3rd Division, which was divided into two groups: J and F. Each was made up

of one infantry regiment, one reserve regiment, one tank company and border guard units. Group J was to advance from Kuusamo, and take Kestenga while Group F (at Suomassalmi) was to attack and capture Ukhta.

While the Finnish 6th Division crossed the frontier on 1 July at midnight, the German corps did not inaugurate its offensive, with a customary Stuka attack, until 16:00 hours. But in summertime the Arctic is bathed with sunlight both day and night. In addition, the heat was a scorching 80 degrees Fahrenheit (27 degrees Celsius), which caused forest fires (set alight by the artillery salvoes and the dive-bombers) and there were swarms of stinging mosquitoes. The German advance was stopped in its tracks by the Soviet border fortifications and poor battle prowess of the SS troops, earning Demelhuber a sarcastic "congratulation" from von Falkenhorst for the behaviour of his troops. During 2–3 July, the 169th Division made several attempts to break the deadlock. On 4 July XXXVI Corps' head-quarters staff were astonished to see terrified motor-ized SS troops fleeing down the road, claiming that they had encountered Russian tanks and that the bridges across the Kemi River had to be blown. For Feige and von Falkenhorst, this simply confirmed once and for all that the SS troops were wholly unreliable. Feige ordered the 6th Division to advance northwards toward Kayrala. On 6 July the 169th Division, sup-ported by two panzer companies, began attacking and by midday had reached Salla. The two armoured com-panies lost most of their tanks but had knocked out 16 Soviet ones within an hour. By 17:00 hours the town was captured, but the Germans were immediately thrown back by fierce Russian counterattacks. It was only through a Russian retreat eastwards that Salla was cap-tured by the morning of 8 July. Most of the Soviet 122nd Division had escaped, but had left most of its artillery behind and all its 50 tanks were destroyed. The corps was proud to have captured Salla and inflicted such a stinging defeat upon the enemy, but von Falkenhorst commented sarcastically that the positions that SS *Nord* had confronted could have been taken by raw recruits (von Falkenhorst's comments were quite unfair). While SS *Nord* pursued the Soviet 122nd Division towards Lampela, the 169th Division turned east to prevent the enemy from making a stand at Apa and Lake Kuola.

Although it was not ideal tank country, tanks were used on the Arctic Front. Here, a pair of Soviet T-60 light tanks break cover followed by a T-26 medium tank.

In the early morning on 9 July, units from the 169th Division reached within 2.4km (1.5 miles) of Kayrala but were thrown back by strong Russian counterattacks. The Soviets had the 122nd Division behind the lakes, the narrows between them were held by the 104th Rifle Division while the 1st Armoured Division was positioned around Allakurtti. It was a formidable array of units. The corps wanted simply to force the Russians out of the defensive line, but headquarters wanted it to make a thrust much deeper: to the east of the Nurmi River. On 16 July von Falkenhorst arrived at the front to inquire what was holding up the advance, and was told that the German troops were unfamiliar with and intensely disliked forest fighting. By comparison, both the Finns and Russians were much better at it. Unimpressed with these "excuses", von Falkenhorst would report to Hitler that XXXVI Corps was completely "degenerate". His conclusion was that the terrain was fine, the roads, compared to what Dietl confronted, were veritable boulevards and that he saw troops lolling about in hammocks when they should have been working or fighting. Von Falkenhorst concluded he would order Feige to get a move on or he would find a new commander. Yet again von Falkenhorst, who was not a frontline commander, trivialized the corps' problems. For example, the troops he found "lolling" were in fact resting from work carried out on the roads – work carried out at night to avoid the heat and mosquitoes that were present during daytime. During 27 and 29 July, the corps made two separate and desperate attacks against the Soviets but without result. By 30 July XXXVI Corps had advanced 20.8km (13 miles) and lost 5500 troops in the process. The 169th Division had been reduced to 9782 officers and men after suffering almost 3300 casualties.

THE FINNISH ADVANCE

What must have been especially galling for the Germans was that their Finnish allies had made such good progress farther south. General Siilasvou's thrust in Lapland was spearheaded by Group J, which faced the Soviet 54th Division, and which was equally divided between holding both Ukhta and Kestenga. Group F had pushed on to the Vyonitsa (Vuoninnen) River, the point of convergence between Groups J and F. Here it was bogged down for nine days (10–19 July) in destroying encircled Soviet units. On 18 July Buschenhagen visited the Finnish III Corps' headquarters, and was astonished to find that Siilasvuo's corps had advanced over 64km (40 miles) through some of the worst possible terrain and was still going strong. (It must have depressed Buschenhagen to see the Finns performing so well in comparison with untrained and unseasoned German troops.) Group J faced a 12.8km- (8-mile-) long canal between Lakes Pya and Top, which was well defended. But on 30 July the Finns began to move one battalion by boat across the canal to land in the Russians' rear. It took them five days to defeat the Russians.

On 7 August the Finns reached Kestenga, which was desperately defended by scratch Soviet forces made up of 500 forced labourers and 600 headquarters staff

German Gebirgsjäger in northern Finland at the end of 1941. Dietl's mountain troops were well-trained and led, but conditions and the enemy combined to prevent them taking Murmansk.

Red Army casualty evacuation in the depths of winter on the Finnish Front was a matter or urgency, not comfort. The difficulty of controlling the towed sled over uneven snow at speed necessitated the use of highly skilled skiers.

Following their experiences in the Winter War, the Red Army made much greater use of ski troops from 1941. The sled-mounted machine gun is the Soviet version of the classic 1910 Maxim gun.

from the Fourteenth Army. Group J followed the railway east of Kestenga but was now held up by stiffening Soviet resistance. On 14 August came the news that the Russians were transferring the 88th Rifle Division from Archangel, and during the next week resistance increased. On 25 August Siilasvuo informed von Falkenhorst that it would be impossible to take Loukhi in a rapid thrust, and so he requested an additional Finnish division – experienced in forest fighting – before he advanced, as his six Finnish and three SS battalions faced 13 Soviet ones.

Group F had made no headway against Ukhta while J, even when supported by SS *Nord*, was unable to push farther east. The Finno-German troops retired to Kestenga when the Soviet 88th Rifle Division and the Independent "Grivnik" Brigade attacked their forward positions. On 14 September the German High Command agreed to halt the Ukhta offensive and shift the emphasis towards Group F. The attack in this sector began on 30 October, and in two days it had trapped one Soviet regiment. Siilasvuo, instead of pressing on with the offensive, insisted on reducing this pocket of resistance before he advanced. This earned him a sharp reprimand from the German High Command, but he knew that Mannerheim wanted him to go over to the defence. The "mopping up" was completed by 13 November, by which time Siilasvuo's men had killed 3000 Russians and captured 2600. Three days later Siilasvuo called off a planned offensive despite his own officers' and German complaints. Von Falkenhorst believed Siilasvuo – a commander who did not shun his duties or the opportunity to defeat the Russians – had acted upon Mannerheim's direct orders. The Finns did not wish to get too deep into Germany's war with Stalin, which could anger the USA.

FURTHER GERMAN ASSAULTS

Meanwhile, XXXVI Corps' headquarters had ordered its two divisions to prepare for new offensives. German military prestige was at stake – they had to show the Finns they could take the Murmansk line and inflict serious defeats upon the Soviet "Untermensch" (sub-humans). But this was not sound military thinking. The season was growing late, the troops were tired and there were no new reinforcements available. The Finnish 6th Division was to do the job, while the German 169th Division was stripped of materiel and troops. Feige believed (quite rightly) that von Falkenhorst was unsympathetic to his plight and trivialized his requests for reinforcements. Their relations soured still further. Nevertheless, the 6th Division attacked with typical Finnish determination and reached Lake Nurmi. Russian defences collapsed and the fleeing Soviets abandoned both vehicles and equipment. However, Soviet combat troops managed to escape along an undetected road that was not closed by the 6th Division until 25 August. Two days later the Russians were forced to fall back to the Tuutsa River. Troops from the 169th Division crossed the river on a footbridge overlooked by the otherwise diligent Russian sappers. After savage fighting the Russians suddenly abandoned Allakurtti, and the 169th could advance to the Voyta River where the pre-1940 Soviet border fortifications were situated. These fortifications were manned by four infantry regiments and a single motorized regiment. Furthermore, on 15 September 8000 reinforcements from Kandalaksha moved up to the frontline.

On 6 September, an attack by four German regiments failed and the day after a massive rainstorm made it impossible to advance. For two days the fighting was bogged down around Hill 386, which was only taken by 10 September. The Russians fought stubbornly and even retook another height (Hill 366), while the German regiments refused to advance until Feige intervened in person. The Russians organized their defences along a line from Lake Verkhneye Verman to Tolvand – the so-called VL or Verman Line. It was held by the 104th and 122nd Divisions, which were restored to 80 percent strength by some 5000 reinforcements. Farther east, volunteer and forced labour combined had built another three defence lines to cover the approaches to Kandalaksha. XXXVI Corps was now exhausted and had suffered, since 1 September, 9000 casualties. The 169th Division was no longer even in shape to perform its defensive tasks. Yet in spite of this, on 22 September the German High Command ordered the corps to prepare for another offensive in October. That unrealistic order was luckily rescinded on 8 October.[28]

THE VERDICT

Von Falkenhorst had been a far from satisfactory commander, and both Feige and Dietl were highly critical of his style of command. Von Falkenhorst had lost the confidence of his subordinates and his superior, Hitler, in equal measure and was replaced as commander of the newly styled Lapland Army by Dietl. Dietl himself had excellent credentials as a commander, personal charm and was very popular among both the Finnish and German troops. But Dietl questioned his ability to control such a far-flung army, and disliked the bureaucracy that such a post entailed. He faced an uphill task if he was, as Hitler hoped, to deliver a second miracle like that at Narvik back in 1940.[29]

Let us look at the overall results of the 1941 campaign in the far north and how well, or otherwise, the different armies had performed. The Russians had been thrown on the defensive and had performed, as compared to the disasters on the main front against the German army groups, commendably. The Red Army's performance during the 1941 campaign was a huge improvement compared to the Winter War, despite its numerical inferiority, lack of tanks and heavy equipment. The Soviets had used the terrain to great effect, especially in the blocking of roads, building strongpoints and the stubborn defence of fortified positions. Unlike the routs on the main front, the Russians conducted a well-led fighting retreat that delayed their enemies' advance by blowing bridges, laying well-placed minefields and booby traps. The Russians had

The Red Army made extensive use of mortars on all fronts, as their ease of use made them ideal infantry support weapons. The large base-plate is clearly visible on the back of the last man in the file.

retained control of most of Karelia and the Murmansk line, and Murmansk remained open to receive Allied aid in ever-increasing amounts.

The Finns could also be satisfied with achieving their relatively limited and modest strategic goals. The advance had been surprisingly fast, but had made the Finnish columns (like the Soviet ones during the Winter War) vulnerable to flank attacks and ambushes. Unlike the enemy, the coordination between artillery and infantry was quite poor in the Finnish Army. Often the infantry would begin their attacks from too far behind the lines or well after the artillery barrage had ended, which allowed the Russians to prepare their defences. The Finns lacked heavy equipment, had no experience of motorized "Blitzkrieg" warfare as operated by their German allies, and the strains of the long Karelian offensive had told on both troops and officers.[30]

But it was the Germans who had least reason to be satisfied with the results of the 1941 campaign. Dietl had failed to capture Murmansk – a major contribution to the failure of the Germans to defeat the USSR. Feige had also failed to reach either Loukhi or Kandalaksha, thus leaving the vital Murmansk railway in Soviet control, which not only kept Murmansk open but enabled the Soviets to exploit their inner and superior lines of communication. It was a huge strategic setback.

But how did it come about? Firstly, Hitler had not given his commanders sufficient numbers of troops or support because he retained too many of these needlessly in Norway. The Führer compounded this mistake by giving these inadequate forces not a single goal that might have been achieved had the German forces been concentrated. The result was that neither of the strategic goals were achieved. The Germans had furthermore totally underestimated the problems of fighting an Arctic war. Their troops, even the Mountain Jägers, were inadequately prepared for the rigours of the climate or terrain. The German High Command, which always looked upon the Arctic campaign as an irritating

Warmly clad and effectively camouflaged, a group of Russian infantrymen assume martial positions for the camera in this propaganda shot.

Red Army tanks and infantry make an attack at the end of 1941. The Soviets on the Finnish Front generally fought with skill and courage.

sideshow, had furthermore underestimated the Red Army's fighting potential. With the railway and White Sea ports at their backs, the Russians could reinforce and shift their forces with an ease denied to the Germans, who had to rely upon completely inadequate road, rail and sea communications. In fact, the Arctic campaign was further removed from the Fatherland than Rommel's Afrika Korps, and Dietl was to share the same problems as his colleague in North Africa: poor supplies, lack of support, a strong enemy and an atrocious environment in which to fight.

One has to conclude that the campaign was flawed from the start, and it was a miracle that Dietl and Feige's men performed as well as they did. Few would disagree that the use of such élite troops as the mountain Jägers in such a job was a waste of fine fighting troops that could have been put to better use elsewhere.

Chapter 4

STALEMATE

ON THE

FROZEN FRONT

As both sides settled down to a desultory campaign in Finland after the end of 1941, the Germans found that the climate and environment in which they had to fight were very harsh. The enemy was the least of their problems.

Following the dramatic and bloody events of 1941, the next three-and-a-half years were to be almost uneventful by comparison. The frontline literally and figuratively froze, as events elsewhere took precedence over this virtually forgotten sector of the Eastern Front.

The Soviet counteroffensive at Moscow was a signal that Hitler's war against the USSR was by no means either a foregone conclusion nor a walkover for the Germans. The Soviet attacks continued well into 1942 all along the front.

On 1 January 1942, the Russians attacked the Finnish Front at Kriv and Maaselkä Stations. While

Red Army infantry scout forward on the Finnish Front during January 1942. These soldiers are well equipped for fighting in the cold, with white oversuits and padded gloves.

the Finnish 8th Division blocked them at Maaselkä, a large hole was torn in the front at Kriv, through which Soviet troops poured. During 5 January both Poventsa and Suurlahti fell to the Russians. The question was whether the Finns would have the strength to hold Karhumäki – the main town and railhead in this sector. It did not seem likely, since by 10 January a Russian brigade had cut the road between Karhumäki and Poventsa. However, during the night of 10–11 January, Finnish artillery (both heavy and field) pounded the Russian positions prior to a counterattack that threw the Soviets back. Those Russian troops that had created a bulge at Kriv were surrounded by the Finns in a "motti" and crushed by the combined strength of the 8th Division and 3rd Jäger Brigade. By the end of February the front was restored to its initial position prior to the Russian offensive.

The Finns themselves decided to make a limited but deep cut through the Russian lines. Detachment M (of two battalions) attacked through the porous Russian lines north of Seesjärvi, towards the Russian station at Maj-Guba on the Murmansk line. A supply depot was blown up and the traffic on the railway was temporarily interrupted. Otherwise the raid, a 150km (93-mile) round trip, did not cause much damage to the enemy, but did deter the Russians from launching a new offensive. The Russians' own raid on Klimetski Island on the west side of Lake Onega ended with a withdrawal.[1]

THE FINNS REORGANIZE

These Soviet operations did not interrupt Mannerheim's reorganization of the army. The Karelian Army was disbanded, Heinrichs was returned to his staff duties and 100,000 troops were discharged. To the Germans, the Finns seemed prepared to return to a state of complete inactivity while they were lumbered with the heavy task of defeating the enemy on their own. That impression must have been reinforced by Mannerheim's refusal to get involved in the siege of Leningrad. In February 1942, Dietl suggested a combined operation whereby the Finns would take Sorokka/Belomorsk on the White Sea and the Lapland Army would be placed under Mannerheim's personal command.

Mannerheim politely rejected Dietl's suggestions. But he agreed to combined operations in the Gulf of Finland. General Pajari's 18th Division was ordered to occupy the Russian-held islands in the bay. On 27 March three battalions crossed the ice and attacked Gogland (Suursaari), which was held by 600 Russian troops. It was conquered by the following evening, and the Russians lost 27 precious aircraft trying to hold it. On 1 April, the smaller island of Tytääsaari was captured and then handed over to a German garrison.[2]

Farther north the Germans had not expected a Soviet spring offensive, and when it did come, in April 1942, they were caught unawares. The Soviet Stavka hoped to take back some territory – to broaden the security zone west of the Murmansk line – before the spring thaw, which would preclude any German counterattack.

A Soviet ski patrol considers breaking cover. Although the Arctic Front was heavily forested, any open ground posed considerable hazards, even for troops as well camouflaged as these, not least from snipers.

On 24 April, the Finnish III Corps was attacked by the Soviet 23rd Guards Division and the 8th Ski Brigade. Two days later the Russians had broken the corps' front and Dietl realized that this was no small local offensive that could be contained by the forces at hand: the Russians were determined to crush the corps and capture Kestenga. He therefore sent reinforcements (one tank and one infantry battalion) to Siilasvuo's assistance.

On 27 April, however, his own front was attacked by the Russians. The 10th Guards Division attacked the German 6th Division while the 14th Rifle Division made a diversionary attack. During the night, the 12th Marine Brigade landed on the western, German-held shore of Litsa Bay. Dietl had been taken completely by sur-

*Not the Russian equivalent of
Father Christmas but part of a
Soviet supply column.
Although the local population
did their best to conserve their
reindeer herds, both the
Wehrmacht and the Red Army
conscripted them in large
numbers.*

prise by the Soviet onslaught, but was saved by an unusually heavy snowstorm that curtailed operations until early May.

Along the Kestenga Front the 8th Ski Brigade had made a wide sweep around the Finnish lines to cut Siilasvuo's supply route, and by 5 May it had reached the main road. Its offensive, however, ran out of steam in the swamps north of Kestenga. In the following two days Finnish and German troops annihilated the brigade, which lost all but 367 of its troops. Off the Arctic coast, incessant Stuka attacks upon its maritime lines of communications forced the 12th Marine Brigade to withdraw on 14 May. Three days later, the Germans had regained their original frontline on the Litsa River.

The spring thaw that came earlier farther south had postponed Siilasvuo's counterattack until 15 May, and it was not until 21 May that Soviet defences had been breached. This was due to the Finns being bogged down completely, and the Russians having built elaborate and strong field fortifications to delay the Finno-German offensive. Despite this success, on 23 May Siilasvuo infuriated Dietl by calling a halt to the offensive. Dietl, like Siilasvuo's German subordinates, believed the Finnish general's decision to be politically motivated. Probably Siilasvuo, experienced forest fighter that he was and knowing the Russians better than Dietl, had made a prudent decision. The Russians had lost 15,000 men on the Litsa and 8000 in the Kestenga sector, while Finno-German losses were respectively 3200 and 2500.

As the Russians had sent the 152nd (Ural) Division, some 20,000 reinforcements in all, to this front, Dietl expected an offensive that in fact never came. He could now deal with the Finns, whom he had come to distrust, and on 3 July XVIII Mountain

In the absence of tracked vehicles both sides reverted to man and horsepower. These Russian drivers are dressed in three-quarter length sheepskin coats, which afforded excellent protection against the elements.

Corps (General Franz Böhme) replaced the Finns in the Kestenga sector. The Soviet spring offensive had revealed ominous cracks in the Finno-German "alliance" that were only to widen over the next two years. Thus the last offensive operations on the Arctic and Finnish Fronts ended on a sour note.

The far north, the scene of such dramatic military action during the previous year, now fell silent. During the rest of 1942 events in the south, in the Caucasus, Kuban and along the Volga, were to decide the outcome of the war on the Eastern Front.

In the Litsa and Kestenga sectors the Germans settled down to a more leisurely and humdrum existence. The Litsa Front was described in the following terms by one author:

"As a result of the stalemate, the areas behind the German frontlines assumed the appearance of well-organized depots nestling snugly in an Arctic 'wonderland'. Ammunition dumps, supply centres, canteens, bakeries, charcoal kilns, hospitals and rest camps were established, and in some parts of the front the solders found it possible to supplement their rations – already on the highest scale provided by the Wehrmacht – by hunting, fishing, pig rearing and vegetable growing." [3]

These ample rations included five cigarettes per day and regular packets of tobacco and fruit rolls. Three times a week a tot of rum or schnapps was issued, and every Sunday a bar of chocolate was given to each soldier.

UNIFORMS FOR WINTER WARFARE

Compared to many other sectors of the Eastern Front the Arctic fighters were taken good care of, but it was a minimum compensation for fighting in such atrocious conditions. During the winter there was almost complete and perpetual darkness, with icy storms from the North Pole and temperatures that could plunge down to 50 degrees below zero. To survive the troops needed not only a heavy diet but warm clothing. The troops were issued with fur-lined white overalls, heavy fur-lined boots, 2–3 pairs of woollen socks and balaclava helmets. The Germans were also well equipped with skis: excellent laminated Norwegian skis with Kandahar bindings for each man (the Russians had to make do with a primitive pair of wooden skis for every five men). While the Austrians and Bavarians seemed to have been born skiers, German troops from other parts of the Third Reich had to go through a thorough training course before they became acceptable skiers.[4]

Overall, the Arctic was the most uncongenial and unpleasant place in which to fight a modern war. As if the winters were not bad enough, the summers were no better and one Arctic fighter, Oberjäger Lamm, believed them to be even worse. It was impossible, claimed Lamm, to dig trenches without dynamiting the ground first because of the permafrost on the tundra, while the damp rising from the innumerable lakes and swamps covered leather in mould, mildewed textiles (including constantly damp uniforms) and caused wood to rot.

Protected by somewhat rudimentary camouflage, this Red Army signals team keeps communications open. The production of radio sets only began to match demand in 1944–45.

But these were minor inconveniences compared to an enemy far worse than the Russians: thick clouds of mosquitoes and other flying pests that bred in their millions in those same swamps and lakes. These pests made life for the Germans (and the Russians and Finns) a total misery. One German soldier not unnaturally concluded that if there was a Hell on Earth for a fighting soldier then that had to be the Arctic wilderness of Lapland.[5] Farther south the Germans had to contend with the same bloodthirsty insects, but they had one additional item that bred melancholy and gloom: an almost endless, almost impenetrable belt of forest that was damp, humid and dark like a regular jungle.

To relieve the boredom, bordering in some cases on the suicidal, the German High Command was forced to offer the troops long leaves of absence. A three-week leave meant, due to the distances and transport complications involved, an absence from the front of over two months. Those who remained were introduced by the

The crew of a 107mm PBHM model 1938 mortar load their weapon. The Red Army placed much faith in the flexibility and potency of mortars.

local Finns to the healthy, if somewhat dubious, "pleasures" of the Finnish steam sauna and icy dips into frozen lakes. The less hardy could read the *Lapland Courier* or listen on the wireless to programmes from the studios at Kirkenes and Petsamo.

On the Finnish Front the problems were the same, but the Finns were more accustomed to them than the Germans and knew how to alleviate the problems. Unlike the Germans the Finns were closer to home, which enabled them to get long furloughs and leaves of absence. At any given time, for example, over 10 percent of the troops would be home on leave. This was established policy and encouraged by the High Command. The troops were desperately needed behind the lines to help with the harvest and farming work. They could keep in touch with loved ones at home by mail, by telegrams or even by phone: privileges not available to the Germans.

During 1942 the Finns built more permanent lines of defence. The trenches and dugouts were all lined with logs, while behind the actual frontline the Finns built so called "korsu": wooden log cabins covered with a deep, solidly packed layer of soil. In 1942 these lacked most amenities, but by 1944 they contained bunk beds, tables, open fires, chairs, windows, oil lamps and even electric light. The Finns, like the Russians, were adept at building field fortifications, laying minefields and barbed wire defences. They took on the same permanence as the German sector of the front.

FORTIFICATION SYSTEMS

Fortifications were not, like the Western Front during World War I, a continuous line of trenches, bunkers and wire stretching from the Baltic Sea to the Arctic Ocean. From the Isthmus to the northern edge of Lake Onega there was a continuous frontline where a division held sectors of 15–40km (9–24 miles) each, depending on how vulnerable the sector was. Here, the Finns built additional and stronger fortifications behind the frontline. North of Onega the frontline was thinly held by fortified strongpoints held by individual platoons every 1 to 10km (0.6 to 6.2 miles), again depending on circumstances. The huge gaps in between were patrolled regularly to keep an eye on the enemy. Should a strongpoint be attacked, then troops would be rushed to its assistance drawn from patrols, other strongpoints or the battalion reserves. But it could take hours, in some cases half a day, for these reserves to reach a strongpoint under attack.

Stalemate on the Finnish Front did not mean there was complete torpor reigning there. On the contrary, both sides showed great skill at skirmishing, sniping and raiding. The Russians were masters of these arts, but the Finns soon copied their adversary's tactics and proved as skilled at this form of fighting as their former masters.

Using the excellent natural cover to best effect, the Russians were without doubt brilliant at sniper warfare. Their snipers were extremely cunning in concealing themselves, incredibly patient in waiting for their quarry and used every available trick to lure their victims to their death. One especially effective trick – given the absence of women in Finnish frontline units – was for female Russian soldiers to strip

off and show off their goodies to their sex-starved enemy. Invariably the Finns would crawl up to the lip of the trench and peer over the edge. Many a Kalle or Charlie (the Russian nickname for the Finnish soldier) paid a high price for his erotic curiosity. But the Finnish countermeasures proved both deadly and effective. They built wooden covers, blinds, palisades and used trench periscopes instead of direct observation with binoculars. They also trained and equipped their own snipers, whose job was to pick out and eliminate the Soviet ones.

Another art of war the Russians proved adept at was skirmishing. Using small, mobile units composed of hand-picked troops, they would strike the Finnish lines where they were least expected. The Russians would usually attack at night and especially when their movements could be concealed by snow, fog or rain. Pioneers would silently cut the barbed wire fence and sappers would then clear a path through the minefields. Then artillery and howitzers would suddenly open fire on the Finnish lines, while an assault group poured through the gap created by the sappers. Sentries and outposts would be captured and returned to the Russian lines for some heavy handed interrogations at the hands of the political commissars. The Finns made the tactical mistake of placing their troops' resting quarters – the *korsu* – at too great a distance from the actual frontline trenches. So by the time the alarm had been raised and the Finns had rushed to the rescue of their comrades, the Russians would already

Rest and relaxation, always an important part of servicemen's and women's lives. The Russian celebration here is apparently in honour of the officer at the far end of the table.

Obviously aware of Napoleon's maxim that an army marches on its stomach, this Russian cook is clearly happy in his work. The rations provided by the Soviet authorities were basic but plentiful.

be well on their way back to friendly territory. By changing their tactics and copying the Russians, the Finns managed to reduce the Russian raiders' effectiveness. They also proved skilled themselves at raiding Russian positions, after learning their lessons the hard way.

Sometime such minor incidents could escalate into something more serious and deadly. At Kriv – where a battle had taken place in January – the Russians had, since the middle part of August, kept up relentless skirmishing against the Finnish lines, which exhausted the frontline troops. On this sector the Finnish 3rd Brigade faced an entire Soviet division – the 289th, supported by four regiments from the 367th Division. At dawn on 15 September the Russians unleashed a full-scale offensive against the Finnish lines and caught the defenders unawares. Their position fell to the Russians. The day after the Finns had retaken their positions, but at a heavy price. Then the Russians, using artillery and for the first time Katyusha rocket launchers, sent in yet another offensive. The rocket launchers' infernal noise and concentrated firepower terrified and confused the Finns, who fell back in panic. The brigade commander, finally realizing this was no mere raid, threw in artillery and committed his entire 4th Battalion to battle. By 18 September the Russians had finally been repelled, but the offensive had proven the effectiveness of this new Soviet "wonder weapon". This knowledge would be put to good use at a later date.[6]

THE PARTISAN WAR

The forests of Karelia, thinly held by Finnish troops, proved ideal partisan country. The Russians had been using partisan warfare against their numerous invaders since the days of Napoleon, and it was an integral part of Soviet military strategy since the Russian Civil War (1918–21). Then it had played a key role in the communist victory over the White Russians. But during the 1930s Stalin's purges had removed the most experienced and capable partisan commanders, either to a premature death or a lingering one in the Gulag death camps. Hence when Barbarossa was unleashed the Russians lacked bases, equipment and commanders to create a partisan army behind the enemy's lines. The efforts of the partisans in 1941 proved quite ineffective, mainly due to Stalin's mistakes and lack of forethought. That it had revived or survived at all by 1942 was to a great extent due to Hitler's monumental mistake of not treating the "conquered" Slavs as allies but as cattle to be mistreated at the whim of their supposed conqueror. The civilian population turned on their former German "liberators" with a vengeance.[7]

Stalin appointed General Panteleimon Ponomarenko to command the Partisan Army from his GHQ in Moscow. Major-General Semion Vershinin became commander of the Karelian Partisan District, where in total 16 partisan units were set up in 1942. Three units were transferred from Archangel and operated out of Kandalaksha. The partisans were set up and controlled by the Communist Party and not the Red Army. But they were supported and supplied by the latter in cooperation with the NKVD (secret police) border authorities.[8]

The partisans were kept on a very tight leash so they would not desert or even turn their weapons against the Soviet authorities. They were also strongly admonished to perform valiant feats of arms or they would be liable to extreme forms of punishment: torture, deportation, reprisals against relatives or even execution. Slackers and cowards were dealt with harshly and without pardon. The partisans were therefore caught between two fires. On the one hand a harsh enemy, and on the other their own side's murderous demands.

Ambush! A Red Army 45mm Model 37 anti-tank gun waits for its prey. It was a derivative of the German 37mm anti-tank gun but could fire high-explosive shells in an infantry support role.

One of the most successful of the Karelian partisan units was commanded by Captain Faddei Zurih and his political commissar, Vassili Perttunen, who was a native Karelian. Karelians and Finns in Soviet exile were not trusted by the Soviet authorities to fight against their compatriots on the other side of the lines. Zurih, as a non-native and a former NKVD border guard, could not only be trusted but knew the territory his unit "Red Partisan" (*Krazni Partisan*) was to operate in inside and out. The captain's military training, leadership and practical experience proved invaluable, and the unit could point to 30 deep operations inside Finnish-held areas.

In the Murmansk region the local party leadership had planned to set up 12 partisan units in 1941, but since the Germans never occupied the city only two units were actually activated on 13 August 1942: "Polar Bolshevik" and "Soviet Murmansk". The former was commanded by the feared and legendary Alexander Smirnov, a.k.a. "Captain Karoka". Smirnov was a cunning and skilled partisan commander who showed no mercy to Finns or Germans, be they military or civilian. Smirnov's unit was operational until October 1944, making 13 deep raids up to 250–300km (155–186 miles) inside enemy held territory. Its base camp, some 20km (12.4 miles) from the Finnish border, was located at Hill 137.2 on an island in the middle of Lake Not – 130km (80 miles) west of Murmansk. Smirnov and his partisans proved a deadly threat to the Finnish settlements in the wilderness of Lapland.

On 24 September Smirnov's unit attacked the tiny hamlet of Viiksamo, which did not have any Finnish border troops to protect it. It was out-of-the-way hamlets and isolated farms, without any form of military protection, that were most exposed to partisan attacks. At Viiksamo the partisans looted the farms of food and valuables. They were about to massacre the inhabitants when a truck filled with Finnish frontier troops arrived and the partisans retreated into the forests.

In January 1943 Smirnov's unit, which had combined with Sergei Kurojedov's *Sovietski Murmansk* for a deep raid into the Petsamo Corridor, did not escape that lightly from the enemy. Having attacked transport convoys and carried out various forms of sabotage, the partisans were set upon and chased by German and Finnish

The waterways that intersected the area and the stable nature of the Arctic Front allowed troops on both sides to keep relatively clean, always a boost for morale and hygiene. These are Red Army troops.

Following the thaw, streams become rivers, and rivers torrents. To ensure vital communications, much effort and energy was expended to keep telephone landlines operative, as is being done here.

ski troops. For the next 19 days the pursuers kept harassing the retreating partisans relentlessly despite the freezing cold and blinding snowstorms. Unable to light fires that would attract the enemy, the partisans were forced to sleep in foxholes where many of them either froze to death or later had to have limbs amputated through frostbite. Only eight partisans returned unscathed.

In August of the same year Smirnov was ordered by Major Betkovsky, the commander of the Murmansk Partisan District, to attack the Arctic Highway inside the Corridor. His orders were to spread general mayhem by killing enemy troops, organizing ambushes and blowing up bridges and vehicles. On 6 August Smirnov set out with 53 men and detached 17 of them to attack the highway while the rest, led by himself, attacked the Finnish village of Yliluiro, which was guarded by a 12 Finnish troops. The partisans very quickly overwhelmed Yliluiro's scant defences and its "garrison". The civilians were plundered, beaten up and in several cases killed.[9] It was deliberate Soviet policy to attack the civilian population to spread fear in the frontier region. The highway detachment managed to blow up a bridge and ambush a post bus: its driver and passengers, including the Bishop of Oulu, were murdered.

It was no wonder the Finns wanted to get their hands on "Karoka" and exact vengeance upon Smirnov and his men. Unlike the Germans, who had no obligation to defend the civilian population, this was not so with the Finns who were frustrated by these deadly pinpricks. The Finns were hampered by their own "gentlemanly" approach to war, and were both shocked and totally unprepared for the enemy's partisan warfare. Since an evacuation was deemed to be demoralizing and might encourage further Soviet attacks, the Finnish authorities had to find other ways of dealing with the partisan menace. They set up a special Frontier Protection Corps ("Skyddskåren") to garrison the border villages, hamlets and even individual farms deemed most exposed to attacks. The corps was also to patrol the wilderness and possibly intercept the partisans before they reached their intended target. But the corps was too small and the area it was to protect an empty, huge wilderness without roads and proper communications. In addition, in 1942 the Finns set up Detachment *Sau* (named after the town of Savukoski) with the specific task of hunting partisans. It was a battalion of hand-picked men whose main task was to follow the trails of the partisans, track them and if possible kill them. They moved on foot or by trucks driven by German drivers lent by Dietl for that specific purpose.[10]

The Finnish anti-partisan units could prove effective when the tables were turned and the hunters became the hunted. On 15 June 1942, a Finnish border post (at Kuusiniemi) had discovered that a Soviet partisan brigade, "Puutoinens", of 759 men had entered the wilderness of Pieninkääs. This was a deeply forested and hilly border region where the nearest road suitable for motorized vehicles was 60–70km (37–43 miles) away. Pieninkääs was also generously sprinkled with lakes, streams and huge stretches of low-lying marshlands. Two Finnish platoons managed to fight the partisans to a standstill at the village of Tjasajoki while additional reinforcements from the 12th Border Brigade were sent into the region.

ANTI-PARTISAN ACTIONS

Having located the enemy at the village of Tjasajoki, four Finnish companies attacked the partisans from all four directions. Some 113 partisans were killed, including the brigade's commander. The remainder retreated, hiding the dead and shooting the wounded so they would not fall into Finnish hands. The commissars, to harden the partisans and prevent desertions, claimed the enemy tortured and killed wounded partisans.

The partisans made it to Lake Jolmajärvi where they built primitive wooden rafts, on which they hoped to escape across the lake to the safety of Soviet-held lines. But the Finns had rushed troops and gunboats to Jolmajärvi. The Finns killed and captured most of the partisans. About 70 of the original force of 759 partisans managed to escape back to their own lines. The Finns were genuinely appalled at the Russian profligacy of life, and noted what a waste of good manpower this kind of clumsy operation was.

A Soviet infantry patrol cautiously approaches an isolated sawmill. The soldier to the left is armed with the comparatively rare Tokarev SVT40 automatic rifle, recognizable by its sight and magazine.

By contrast, their own partisan raids into Soviet-held territory were conducted by small regular units of men with limited military targets. Their favourite objective was the Murmansk railway or the trunk line from Belomorsk to Archangel. The Finns created a well-concealed strongpoint near to the intended target. Once they had struck they would then retreat quickly back to their own lines, always being careful to sow numerous mines, booby traps and other explosive devices behind them.[11]

During 1942 and 1943 the Russian partisans proved a minor nuisance, but in 1944 the partisans attacked simultaneously with the massive offensive by the regular Red Army. The combination was to prove almost fatal to Finland's continued existence and the survival of the German Lapland Army.

Chapter 5

THE WAR ON THE ARCTIC CONVOYS

British and American aid to the Soviet Union was channelled across the Arctic Sea, but the hazards were enormous for the cargo ships involved, as German aircraft, submarines and ships based in Norway pounced on the Allied convoys.

The Norwegian campaign was a brilliant tactical success for the Germans, in which initial surprise and air superiority had counterbalanced the importance of British sea power. The invasion had been launched for strategic naval reasons, but the significance and benefits of the operation were tempered by the losses suffered by the Kriegsmarine (German Navy). Germany had gained naval and air bases in Norway ideal for launching raids on British maritime

Allied ships faced many hazards during the trip to Murmansk. Here, a British ammunition ship explodes after being hit by a bomb during a Luftwaffe attack from air bases in Norway.

communications and made the imposition of a naval blockade on Germany more difficult. Yet the losses to the Kriegsmarine meant that its surface strength was effectively crippled for the rest of war, undermining its potential to exploit fully the strategic advantages accrued from the possession of Norway. Meanwhile, the British quietly occupied Iceland, which somewhat lessened the benefits that the Germans had gained by making the route to the Atlantic by the northern passages more difficult. However, after having to guard the 320km (200-mile) Shetland–Bergen gap, the Royal Navy and Royal Air Force (RAF) now had to patrol the 960km (600 miles) of the Icelandic passages.

RAEDER'S PLANS

By the autumn of 1940 the Royal Navy was increasingly stretched. The French defeat and the entry of Italy into the war threatened British control of the Mediterranean, while the Japanese were becoming increasingly aggressive in the Far East. Nonetheless the German Navy remained the main threat. Grand Admiral Erich Raeder, the Commander-in-Chief of the Kriegsmarine, hoped to disperse the Royal Navy's superior strength and with the aid of his U-boat fleet attack and cut Great Britain's vital Atlantic supply lines. The U-boats would force the Royal Navy to concentrate shipping in convoys, and German surface ships would then destroy these convoys. The pocket battleship *Admiral Scheer* broke into the Atlantic in October 1940 and sunk 100,584 tonnes (99,000 tons) of Allied shipping during her five-month cruise. She was followed by the *Admiral Hipper* – now repaired after her clash with the *Glowworm*. The battle cruisers *Scharnhorst* and *Gneisenau* sank or captured 22 merchantmen, totalling nearly 117,856 tonnes (116,000 tons), between January and March 1941. That March losses in the Atlantic to surface raiders, U-boats and aircraft reached the severest thus far, totalling over 355,600 tonnes (350,000 tons).[1] Raeder's strategy appeared to be working.

Furthermore, two large 50,800-tonne (50,000-ton) battleships, *Bismarck* and *Tirpitz*, were nearing completion. Given the strategic situation, the only task Raeder could give the *Bismarck*, which would be ready first, was raiding in the Atlantic. He intended to send her out with the heavy cruiser *Prinz Eugen*, and make

Grand Admiral Erich Raeder, commander of the German Kriegsmarine. He planned to use U-boats and surface ships to destroy Allied convoys in the Atlantic Ocean.

One of Raeder's U-boats. German submarines tended to hang around convoys like wolves around a flock of sheep, waiting for any stray to become separated from the pack.

a simultaneous sortie with the *Scharnhorst* and *Gneisenau* from Brest. British bombing of the *Gneisenau* and the fact that the refit of the *Scharnhorst* would take longer than expected scuppered this plan, but Raeder still sent out the *Bismarck* and *Prinz Eugen* on 18 May 1941. The ships were spotted by the Swedish Navy, and the pro-British Major Törnberg of the Swedish Intelligence Service passed the information to the military attaché of the Norwegian Government-in-Exile, Colonel Captain Roscher Lund. Lund then gave the news to Henry Denham, the British naval attaché in Stockholm, who immediately telegraphed London. The news was confirmed when an RAF Spitfire spotted the *Bismarck* outside Bergen.[2] This started the chain of events which led to the encounter between the German ships and HMS *Hood* and HMS *Prince of Wales*. Although the *Hood* was destroyed in the engagement, the *Bismarck* was damaged and subsequently caught and sunk in the Atlantic. There were important repercussions on German naval strategy from this event.

In spite of British naval superiority, the vessels of the Royal Navy were unable to do much to hamper the iron ore traffic that was now coming from the repaired port of Narvik. Indeed, Norwegian coastal traffic amounted to some 101,600 tonnes (100,000 tons) of shipping.[3]

The German pocket battle-ship Gneisenau *was active against British commerce in the Atlantic. She was decommissioned in July 1942 and her turrets removed for coastal defence.*

Admiral Karl Dönitz speaking to some of his U-boat crews. Dönitz was responsible for developing the pack system whereby U-boats worked in groups to prey on Allied shipping.

The German battleship Bismarck *photographed from the deck of the cruiser* Prinz Eugen.

In an effort to disrupt this trade, damage the Norwegian fish oil industry and give the newly formed Commandos some experience, on 4 March 1941 the Royal Navy landed 500 Commandos at four fishing ports on the Lofoten Islands, causing considerable damage, sinking 18,288 tonnes (18,000 tons) of shipping and capturing code wheels and books for the German Enigma machine. This raid perturbed Hitler considerably.[4]

Of far more strategic importance was the German invasion of the Soviet Union on 22 June 1941. British Prime Minister Winston Churchill immediately offered British aid and pledged to supply the Soviets as far as possible. This meant sending convoys on a 3200km (2000-mile) journey via the North Cape to Russia's only ice-free Arctic port, Murmansk. The first convoy, codenamed Dervish, sailed on 21 August carrying aircraft for the defence of Murmansk. It arrived safely. On 29 September the first of the regular convoys codenamed "PQ" sailed (the return journey was codenamed "QP"). By the end of the year eight convoys had arrived safely, a total of 55 merchant vessels.[5]

The Royal Navy also began operating more aggressively in the Arctic. There were sound strategic reasons for this. Due to the terrible transport infrastructure in northern Norway and Finland, the Germans needed to supply General Dietl's assault on Murmansk by sea. Indeed, during 1942 nearly 6,096,000 tonnes (6 million tons) of materiel were convoyed around the North Cape to Petsamo. Dietl's Arctic campaign was almost entirely reliant on these seaborne supplies.[6] On 30 July 1941, the British launched two costly carrier-borne air attacks on the heavily defended ports of Kirkenes and Petsamo. In August a raid was mounted against Spitsbergen and in December, more spectacularly, two further Commando raids were launched against the Lofotens and Vagsoy. All this added to Hitler's fears that the British were preparing an invasion of Norway.

The advent of the Arctic convoys changed the strategic situation in the north once again. The convoys were of vital importance to the Russians. Once it was clear that they had survived the initial onslaught, the Western Allies – including the United States which had entered the conflict in December 1941 – stepped up efforts to keep the Soviet Union in the war. The Royal Navy was tasked with operations described by its Official Historian as of, "a more exacting and arduous nature than in any other theatre of war."[7] The seas and weather in winter were appalling. During the summer the perpetual daylight aided German reconnaissance and heightened the danger of air attack. The Germans were in possession of excellent sea and air bases in Norway, along the southern flank of a convoy route from which there could be little deviation. There was no doubt where all the strategic and tactical advantages lay. Even so, the Germans did not seriously attempt to interfere with the convoys until early 1942, by which time their forces in Norway had increased dramatically.

SHIFTS IN GERMAN STRATEGY

Three events: the sinking of the *Bismarck*, the Commando raids on Norway and a realization in Berlin that the Arctic convoys were important, all had major effects on German naval strategy. After the loss of the *Bismarck* the German naval staff did not renounce the idea of further surface operations in the Atlantic, and had planned to send the *Tirpitz* out with the *Hipper*. Yet Hitler had been shaken and the Commando raids played on his fear that Great Britain might invade Norway. In November 1941 he decided to send the *Tirpitz* to Trondheim rather than into the Atlantic. Hitler, "convinced that Norway is the 'zone of destiny' in this war", ordered a heavy reinforcement of land and air forces and demanded that "every available vessel be employed in Norway."[8] Hitler also put considerable limits on the use of capital ships, against which Raeder protested in vain.[9]

This was a major shift in German policy and it was further reinforced by Hitler's decision that the *Scharnhorst* and *Gneisenau*, based at Brest, should join the *Tirpitz* in Norway. In an audacious operation in February 1942, the two battle cruisers with the heavy cruiser *Prinz Eugen* returned to German waters via the English Channel, causing considerable embarrassment to the Royal Navy and the RAF. Yet both *Scharnhorst* and *Gneisenau* received serious mine damage, while *Prinz Eugen* was torpedoed off Kristiansand and had to return to port. Only the *Scharnhorst* could join the *Tirpitz* in Norway seven months later. Despite the blow to British pride

The battleship Bismarck *posed a major threat to Allied shipping in the Atlantic in 1941.*

this tactical victory was essentially a strategic withdrawal. As Churchill said to the British parliament, "the threat to our [Atlantic] convoy routes has been driven from this highly advantageous position."[10] He was right: this operation was essentially a renunciation of ocean warfare, and the burden of the Atlantic war was passed almost completely to Admiral Karl Dönitz's U-boat arm.

By early 1942 German naval units in Norway consisted of the *Tirpitz*, the pocket battleships *Lützow* and *Admiral Scheer*, the heavy cruisers *Prinz Eugen* and *Hipper*, the light cruiser *Köln*, five destroyers and twenty U-boats. The main concern of the

British was that the German ships in Norway, particularly the *Tirpitz*, did not break out into the Atlantic. Just after she arrived in Norwegian waters, Winston Churchill described the destruction of the warship as "the greatest event at sea at the present time. No other target is comparable to it." He asserted that "the whole strategy of the war turns at this period on this ship which is holding four times the number of British capital ships paralyzed, to say nothing of the two new American battleships retained in the Atlantic."[11] As a result, the first British bombing missions were launched against the *Tirpitz* in late January 1942.

The Admiral Scheer *fires a salvo at an Allied merchantman. In 1940, the* Scheer *sank thousands of tons of Allied shipping.*

Yet the most obvious use for the *Tirpitz* was against the Arctic convoys, and she made her first sortie on 6 March 1942 against PQ12, which had been spotted by a Focke Wulf 200 reconnaissance aircraft the previous day. *Tirpitz* was spotted by a British submarine and Admiral Tovey, the British C-in-C Home Fleet, providing distant cover with three capital ships and the aircraft carrier HMS *Victorious*, turned towards PQ12 and its sister homeward-bound convoy QP8. On 8 March appalling weather prevented aerial reconnaissance on both sides, and on that day the two convoys, the British Home Fleet and the *Tirpitz* were all within 128km (80 miles) of each other. Admiral Ciliax, German C-in-C Battleships, decided to turn for home. Tovey, aided by Ultra intercepts of German naval traffic, was able to set off in pursuit and launch an air strike from *Victorious* on 9 March.[12] The *Tirpitz* put up a tremendous anti-aircraft barrage against the determined but inexperienced air crews. Two British aircraft were lost and the German ship was able to

The Bismarck *fires at* HMS Hood *during her last battle in May 1941. The loss of the* Bismarck *was a major loss for the Kriegsmarine.*

put safely into Narvik. The close escape caused Raeder to place further restrictions on German surface operations. There were to be no sorties until air reconnaissance had fully determined the strength of the enemy.[13]

Nonetheless, on 14 March 1942 Hitler decided to make the Arctic convoys a strategic target of major importance linked directly to the campaign in Russia, as the Anglo-American deliveries of war supplies were, "sustaining Russian ability to hold out." He declared that "it is necessary that maritime communications over the Arctic Ocean between the Anglo-Saxons and Russians, hitherto virtually unimpeded, should henceforth be impeded."[14] He was right. Apart from the *Tirpitz*'s ineffectual sortie, the only loss suffered by the Arctic convoys was a 5217-tonne (5135-ton) merchantman from PQ7 sunk by Lieutenant Rudolf Schend's *U-134*. But with Hitler's intervention this was about to change. Quite apart from the formidable German surface and submarine units based in Norway, two specialized Luftwaffe anti-shipping units, KG 26 and KG 30, were transferred to the air bases at Bardufoss and Banak.[15]

There were, however, serious limitations placed on naval operations by the critical nature of the German fuel oil shortage. The loss of Soviet oil due to the launching of Barbarossa added impetus to the German drive towards the Caucasian oilfields. The Ploesti oilfields in Romania were the only Axis source of petroleum and also fuelled the Italian fleet, which was dependent on them. Therefore, just as Hitler demanded an increase in surface attacks on the convoys, the German Naval Command had to order that: "All operations are to be discontinued including those by light forces." The Kriegsmarine received only a tenth of its monthly fuel requirement that April. The U-boats were unaffected as they used diesel oil. So from about February 1942 onwards all surface operations were governed by the availability of

Soviet destroyers sail out of Murmansk on their way to meet an Allied convoy in 1941. The Germans attempted to intercept Soviet warships before they linked up with the convoys.

The British assigned aircraft carriers as convoy escorts. These ships are HMS Biter *(left) and* Avenger *(right). The aircraft on the* Avenger *are Hurricanes. Note the heavy seas that were a feature of the Arctic convoy routes.*

fuel. As Wilhelm Meisel, captain of the *Hipper*, despairingly declared: "If we are to achieve anything at all the crippling fuel shortage must be ended forthwith."[16]

Despite these problems German pressure on the convoys was increasing, although it was largely U-boats and aircraft that were doing the damage. PQ13 endured both terrible weather and constant German attack. It was spotted by a BV 138B flying-boat on 28 March. Ju 88s of III/KG 30 attacked throughout the day, sinking two stragglers. In what was described as a "miracle", Rear-Admiral Hubert Schmundt, Flag Officer Northern Waters or "Admiral Arctic", was given specific permission to send out three destroyers from Kirkenes after the convoy: *Z24*, *Z25* and *Z26*, under Captain Pönitz. After picking up a number of survivors from the air attacks, he gained enough intelligence to enable Fritz von Berger's *Z26* to sink a stray freighter on 29 March. *Z26*'s luck did not hold as it encountered the British cruiser HMS *Trinidad* and came under accurate gunfire. *Z26*'s fate would have been sealed had not one of *Trinidad*'s torpedoes not malfunctioned and returned to hit the British ship. *Z26* escaped, only to tangle with the British destroyer *Eclipse*, which inflicted further damage on her before being driven off by *Z26*'s sister ships. The German destroyers did not pursue but took off *Z26*'s crew before the ship slowly sunk. PQ13's ordeal was not yet over, as *U-376* and *U-435* both sank a further merchantman each. Nineteen ships had started with PQ13 and five had been lost. This was a loss rate of over 20 percent, and the British Admiralty was worried that it would get worse given that the days were lengthening and the weather improving. The German naval staff, however, was not happy about the loss of *Z26* in return for only one freighter. Admiral Schmundt was urged to be more cautious in future, much to his chagrin.[17]

PQ14 fared somewhat better. Although attacked by the Luftwaffe on 15 April no ships were hit. The submariners were more successful, and Captain Lieutenant Heinz-Ehlert in *U-403* torpedoed a merchant ship on 16 April. This was the convoy's only loss. By now there were 20 U-boats operating in the Arctic, and Grand Admiral Dönitz transferred these to Schmundt's control, although the Grand Admiral was not convinced that this was the best use of his submarines.[18]

THE ASSAULT ON PQ15

The German effort continued. PQ15, made up of 25 merchantmen with a strong destroyer escort, was spotted by the Luftwaffe on 30 April 400km (250 miles) southwest of Bear Island. The first air attacks did not occur until 2 March but these were "raggedly and poorly executed."[19] The convoy remained under continued surveillance by aircraft and U-boats. In the early hours of 3 May six aircraft from I/KG 26 attacked and although three German aircraft were lost, they managed to sink three ships. The Luftwaffe lost another aircraft the following day. The returning convoys were suffering, too. *Trinidad* had to be scuttled after further bomb damage. Another cruiser, HMS *Edinburgh*, escorting QP11, was hit by two torpedoes from Captain Lieutenant Max Martin Teichert's *U-456* on 30 April. Although the *Edinburgh*'s destroyers prevented Teichert from finishing the ship off, he maintained contact and this prompted Schmundt to send out three destroyers, *Z24*, *Z25* and the *Hermann Schoemann*. They made contact with the convoy on 1 May and made five attempts to attack it, but the aggressive tactics of the escorting destroyers kept them at bay, although a German torpedo sank a Soviet merchantman.

That evening Captain Alfred Schulze-Hinrichs, commanding the operation, decided to go after the *Edinburgh*. The British escorts did their best to keep the German ships at a distance, and a 6in salvo from *Edinburgh* hit the *Hermann Schoemann*. As her captain, Heinrich Wittig, recalled: "that the cruiser with her second salvo managed to hit two such vital points [in the engine room] of our ship was the worst luck that could have overtaken us."[20] His ship was crippled and later had to be scuttled. *Z24*, however, managed a torpedo hit on *Edinburgh* and Rear-Admiral Bonham-Carter ordered that the ship be abandoned. The two German destroyers also scored some telling hits on *Edinburgh*'s escorts, but despite his apparent advantage Schulze-Hinrichs declined to press home his advantage and turned for home. There is some debate over his decision, although on the whole German surface commanders routinely displayed considerable timidity in this theatre. It has been suggested that he mistook a number of British minesweepers for fleet destroyers.[21]

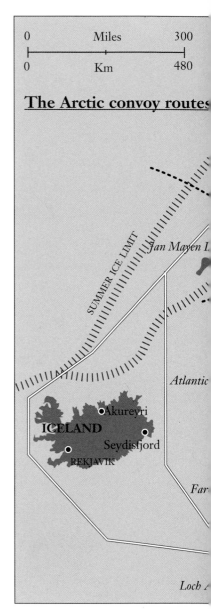

The Arctic convoy routes

The vulnerability of the
Arctic convoys to air and sea
attack can be appreciated
from this map. In summer
the risks to the convoys were
reduced but not eradicated.

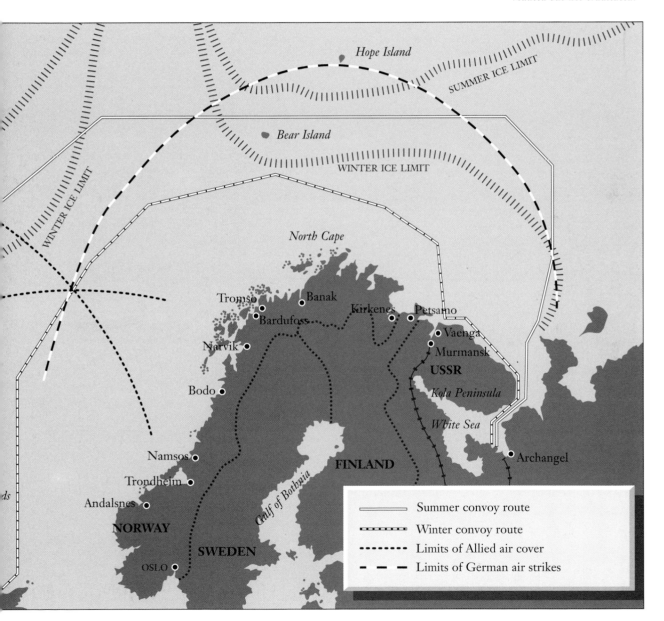

Hope Island

SUMMER ICE LIMIT

Bear Island

WINTER ICE LIMIT

WINTER ICE LIMIT

North Cape

Tromso • Banak
Bardufoss • Kirkenes • Petsamo
Narvik • Vaenga
Murmansk
Bodo • USSR
Kola Peninsula
White Sea

Namsos • FINLAND
Trondheim • Archangel
Andalsnes • *Gulf of Bothnia*
NORWAY
SWEDEN
OSLO •

	Summer convoy route
	Winter convoy route
	Limits of Allied air cover
	Limits of German air strikes

The steady growth of losses, particularly the two cruisers, led Admiral Bonham-Carter to comment:

"Until the aerodromes in north Norway are neutralized and there are some hours of darkness the continuation of these convoys should be stopped. If they must continue for political reasons, very serious and heavy losses must be expected. The force of German attacks will increase, not diminish."[22]

Tovey agreed and wanted the convoys kept small. The British Chief of Staff (COS) committee also had their doubts about the wisdom of continuing. However, Churchill insisted that they continued, claiming that the US and Soviets expected the British to maintain their effort: "Failure on our part to make the attempt would weaken our influence with both our major Allies . . . I share your misgivings but I feel that it is a matter of duty."[23]

So PQ16, of 35 merchantmen, the biggest convoy so far, sailed from Rekjavik on 21 May 1942. It was spotted by an Fw 200 Kondor on the 25th. That evening seven He 111s and eight Ju 88s from III/KG 26 and III/KG 30 attacked and achieved some near misses, although one He 111 was lost to a catapult-launched Hurricane. A second, unsuccessful air attack followed an hour or so later. However, *U-703* sank one

The ill-fated convoy PQ17. This photograph was taken by a German reconnaissance aircraft during the early stages of the convoy's journey to Murmansk.

A merchantman of PQ17 goes down after being hit by a U-boat torpedo. This photograph was taken by the attacking U-boat.

Keeping watch for the enemy as PQ17 makes its way north. The convoy lost a total of 24 ships.

vessel on the morning of 26 May. There was another air attack that day. The main German effort came on the 27th. Over 100 aircraft attacked over a 10-hour period and succeeded in sinking six ships and damaging many more. Although there were a couple more half-hearted attacks over the following days, the worst was over. Despite the losses the British took some consolation from PQ16, given the scale of the German attack. Tovey reckoned that the, "convoy's success was beyond expectation."[24]

This thinking was mirrored by Dönitz, who complained that:

"My opinion as to the small chances of success for U-boats against convoys during the northern summer has been confirmed by the experience with PQ16. Owing to the difficult conditions for attack . . . the result has been one steamer sunk and four probable hits. This must be accounted a failure when compared with the results of the anti-submarine activity for the boats operating [two U-boats seriously and three slightly damaged by depth charges]." [25]

The British were proving capable of dealing with the U-boat and Luftwaffe threat, but the German heavy ships were another matter. It was inexplicable that they had not attacked seriously – the British were not aware of German fuel shortages – and the Admiralty knew that there was no defence against them. British capital ships could not enter the Barents Sea until they were sure that the *Tirpitz* was not making for the Atlantic, and in any case the Barents Sea, filled with U-

The Focke-Wulf Fw 200 Kondor was a long-range reconnaissance and attack aircraft. It was nicknamed the "Scourge of the Atlantic", although the Luftwaffe never had enough of them to have a decisive impact on the Arctic convoys to and from Russia.

boats and in range of German land-based bombers, was too dangerous a place. Essentially the British believed they had no real defence against the *Tirpitz* if she caught a convoy east of Bear Island. All that could be done was to order the convoy to scatter, and as Tovey later said to the Official Historian, if that happened, "it would be sheer bloody murder."[26]

Unfortunately for the British the Germans had decided to attack the next convoy in strength using the *Tirpitz*, *Hipper* and the two pocket battleships based in Norway. When Raeder proposed targeting PQ17 on 15 June, Hitler expressed grave concern about the operation, codenamed *Rösselsprung* (Knight's Move). Fearing the threat of British carrier-borne aircraft he ordered that, "the aircraft carriers must be located before the attack, and they must be rendered harmless by our Ju 88 planes before the attack gets under way."[27] Once more the Führer had placed serious limitations on his naval officers' freedom of action. Even so, Raeder transferred his heavy ships north, although the *Lützow* and three destroyers ran aground outside Narvik. The other ships reached the anchorage at Altenfjord without incident.

RAF reconnaissance showed that their berths at Trondheim were empty and Enigma decrypts indicated that the *Tirpitz* was preparing to put to sea.[28] Dudley Pound, the British Chief of the Naval Staff, well aware of the catastrophe that would occur if the *Tirpitz*, *Hipper*, *Scheer* and, for all he knew, *Lützow* as well caught the convoy, ordered the escort withdrawn and the convoy to scatter.[29] Tovey was convinced it was the wrong decision and believed that determined torpedo-armed escorts would

Torpedo-armed German Heinkel He 111 bombers were used to good effect against the Arctic convoys.

2842

deter the Germans. Pound, however, was not willing to take that risk and chance the total destruction of the convoy, escorts and all. The *Tirpitz* had made her most destructive contribution to the naval war without firing her guns. By her threatened presence she had broken the cohesion of a convoy, something all the U-boats and aircraft in northern Norway had failed to do. When it was clear that the convoy had scattered she turned back to Altenfjord, leaving the slaughter to aircraft and U-boats. Twenty-four ships were lost over the following days, and only 12 made it to Murmansk. As Admiral Otto Schniewind, the fleet commander, commented, *Rösselsprung*, "aptly demonstrated that without some offensive spirit, warlike operations cannot be carried out with hope of success."[30]

GERMAN MORALE PROBLEMS

Nonetheless, there were problems of morale amongst the men of the German surface fleet in Norway. They were hampered by the increasingly restrictive orders and had seen virtually no action. After the scattering of PQ17 Commander Reinicke complained: "They should have let us make one little attack! Heaven knows they could always have recalled us after we had bagged three or four merchantmen. One should not forget the psychological effect on officers and men!" The German heavy ships had been sitting in their Arctic berths for months, enduring occasional British air attack. The crews had seen virtually no action. The climate, particularly in winter, is extremely harsh and the Norwegian ports, some of which were extremely remote, hardly compared to Wilhelmshaven or Kiel, let alone the French west coast ports, and offered very limited diversions for off-duty sailors. Boredom is not good for morale and the officers were well aware of the problem. It is worth quoting Lieutenant Commander Günther Schultz, First Operations Officer Destroyers, at length:

"Here the mood is bitter enough. Soon one will feel ashamed to be on the active list if one has to go on watching other parts of the armed forces fighting, while we, 'the core of the Fleet', just sit in the harbour.

"The ships' commanders have now been waiting for action up here for nearly six months. They tore their hair enough, when we let PQ16 get through. When their men asked quite reasonably why our ships had remained idle, their skippers had to shut them up by talking rubbish . . . Psychologically, it was like letting a bull loose in a china shop."[31]

In an effort to provide some purpose the *Scheer* attempted to intercept a Russian convoy in the Kara Sea in August but failed, and the *Hipper* fruitlessly swept the Barents Sea. Essentially Hitler's caution had paralyzed the fleet, and this was to have a dire effect when it confronted British surface units.

The British Admiralty demanded that the Arctic convoys cease through the summer months, and so PQ18 did not sail until September. Forty merchant ships were assembled, and for the first time an Arctic convoy was given its own local air cover

The German light cruiser Köln *was one of those ships earmarked to attack PQ18, but was not used due to the fears of Hitler regarding naval losses.*

by the inclusion of the escort carrier HMS *Avenger*. An anti-aircraft cruiser, HMS *Scylla*, 16 destroyers and a whole host of corvettes, trawlers and minesweepers completed the convoy's protection. The Home Fleet would provide distant cover. The Germans had also made considerable plans for PQ18, boosted by their success against the previous convoy. The *Scheer*, *Hipper* and the light cruiser *Köln* were moved to Altenfjord. Hitler, as ever, insisted they take no risks, so Raeder cancelled the operation. The experience of PQ17 had convinced the Luftwaffe erroneously that the previous success could be repeated merely by the use of aircraft. Twelve U-boats were sent out, but the main effort would be made by Colonel-General Stumpff's Luftflotte 5. The Germans had assembled a considerable force in northern Norway. Forty-two He 111H-6 torpedo bombers of KG 26 were joined by 35 Junkers Ju 88A-17s, a new Ju 88 modification also capable of carrying torpedoes, flown in specially from France. They would operate in combination with the Ju 88

bombers of KG 30 using a tactic called the *Goldern Zange* (Golden Comb). Mid-level and dive-bombing by KG 30 would break up the cohesion of the British escorts, while low-level torpedo attacks would do the real damage. The Germans were aware that HMS *Avenger* was sailing and Göring ordered that, "the attack against the aircraft carrier must be so violent that this threat is removed." He told his pilots that a victory over PQ18 would be of vital significance to the war against the Soviet Union, as it would deprive the Red Army of important equipment and thus ease the progress of the army at Stalingrad and the drive into the Caucasus.[32]

Captain Lieutenant Max Martin Teichert's *U-456* was the first to spot the convoy as it rounded the southwest corner of Iceland. An Fw 200 picked it up again on 8 September. From then on PQ18 was constantly shadowed by U-boats and long-range reconnaissance aircraft. The U-boats made a number of attacks and two merchantmen were sunk on the morning of 13 September. However, the main attack came that afternoon. The lightly armed Hurricanes flying off *Avenger* were unable to drive off a wave of Ju 88 bombers making a high-level pass. Then came the Golden Comb attack. Twenty Ju 88s of KG 30 carried out a high-level diversionary run, which caused the required degree of disruption. They were followed by the torpedo bombers of KG 26, 28 He 111s in two waves, followed by 18 Ju 88s from Bardufoss. Another 17 Ju 88s of KG 30 from Banak were in support. As Sub-Lieutenant Hughes aboard HMS *Scylla* recalled: "they rose on the horizon, black and repulsive, and they extended far on either side of our view. They came in low on the starboard bow of the convoy and seemed to fill the whole horizon." The convoy

Although very advanced at the time of its design (1933), the Russian Polikarpov I-16 was obsolete by 1942. However, as over 7000 were produced, it was an important machine. Modern aircraft were used on the main fronts, and older types, such as the I-16, were relegated to the Arctic Front.

opened up with everything it had; the Germans came in so low even the 4.7in guns of the destroyers could be brought into action. They pressed their attacks with "suicidal daring [and] flew in amongst the ships, dropping their torpedoes at very close range."[33] Eight ships were lost in a matter of minutes at the cost of only five aircraft.

The next air attack, by Heinkel He 115 seaplanes of the Kriegsmarine flying out of Billefjord, was a very much more half-hearted affair. They showed little of the determination and élan of their Luftwaffe colleagues. They lost two aircraft and were driven off at the cost of one Hurricane. The U-boats continued to make attacks when they had the opportunity. On the 14th *U-457* sank the tanker *Athel Templar* and escaped the pursuing destroyers by diving under the convoy and becoming lost amid the noise of the convoy's propellers. The losses were not all one way: HMS *Onslow* destroyed *U-589*. A specific attack by Ju 88s of KG 26 was made on HMS *Avenger* that day and was broken up with the loss of 11 aircraft. Dive-bombing by KG 30 continued, and in the afternoon another attempt was made on the aircraft carrier, but this also failed to sink her. Five bombers were lost and nine so badly damaged that they were later declared unserviceable. The next day the bombers returned, and by the afternoon seemed content to bomb from above the clouds.[34] The Germans were losing heart. This was confirmed by intercepted radio signals which

Another aircraft used on the Arctic Front against German shipping was the Russian Tupolev SB-2. The camouflage scheme is an interesting one, swirls of colour with few, if any, markings. The capacity was 600kg (1323lb) of bombs stowed internally.

showed increasing disillusionment amongst the German air crews.[35] The tail-end of the battle of PQ18 was played out over the next few days. *Scylla*, *Avenger* and the destroyers detached from the convoy to join the escort of QP14, and were replaced by four Soviet destroyers. Another merchantman was lost, but so were four more German aircraft.

In all 13 merchant ships out of 40 had been sunk, 10 by aircraft and three by U-boats. However, the Germans had lost 41 aircraft and three submarines. The loss of such highly trained crews was a serious blow. The Luftwaffe had misinterpreted its previous success and had made the costly discovery that it could not break up a determinedly defended convoy alone. So PQ18 was an Allied victory, albeit a very expensive one. It also marked a turning point in the Arctic naval war, as the Germans

A destroyer comes alongside the cruiser HMS Scylla *to transfer survivors from a merchantman during the voyage of PQ18.*

would never again be able to muster such numbers of aircraft in the area. Luftflotte 5 was stripped in the wake of the Allied landings in North Africa. When the next convoy sailed for Russia, Luftwaffe resources in northern Norway were limited to long-range reconnaissance aircraft and He 115s.

THE BATTLE OF THE BARENTS SEA

After PQ18, convoys had been suspended due to the demands of the invasion of North Africa on the Home Fleet. However, the Admiralty decided to restart them by sending JW51 in two parts in mid-December. In Germany Hitler remained obsessed with the possibility of an Allied landing in Norway. He sent the now repaired *Lützow* back, adding to the very strong German naval presence there. So taking advantage of this, when, on 30 December 1942, a U-boat reported the British convoy JW51B south of Bear Island, Raeder authorized the *Hipper* and *Lützow* to intercept the convoy. Hitler, apparently ranting that his heavy ships were "uselessly lying about in the fjords", did not contradict the order for once.[36] Operation *Regenbogen* (Rainbow) was intended by its commander, Vice-Admiral Oskar Kummetz, to catch JW51B in a pincer between the *Hipper* and *Lützow*. As they left Altenfjord in the company of six destroyers, true to form, Kummetz received a further signal from Admiral Kluber, Flag Officer Northern Waters, stating that, discretion was to be exercised in the face of an enemy of equal strength owing to the undesirability of submitting cruisers to major risk. Once again the Kriegsmarine was being exhorted to exercise caution.

Contact was made on 31 December. The skilful use of the British destroyer escort forced Kummetz, aboard the vastly superior *Hipper*, away from the convoy. However, his plan was working as the convoy turned towards the south and was now without escort, as this had been committed against the *Hipper*. JW51B was completely at the *Lützow*'s mercy. Targets were sighted 4.8km (3 miles) away (the 11in guns of the *Lützow* had a range of 24km – 15 miles) but her captain, Stänge, chose not to engage claiming that he was hampered by poor visibility. Meanwhile, two British cruisers began to engage the *Hipper* and Kummetz, mindful of his instructions, withdrew having achieved nothing. The Battle of the Barents Sea was over. There were some losses amongst the smaller vessels: the Germans lost a destroyer and the British a destroyer and a minesweeper.

The Admiralty was delighted: light forces had driven off a heavy cruiser and pocket battleship without loss to the convoy. The reaction in Germany was understandably somewhat different. Hitler, angered at having heard the first results of *Regenbogen* via Reuters, told Admiral Kranke, Raeder's representative at the Führer's headquarters, that: "the heavy ships are a needless drain on men and material. They will accordingly be paid off and reduced to scrap. Their guns will be mounted on land for coastal defence." He treated Raeder to an extended diatribe along the same lines six days later. Hitler failed to recognize that it was his own reluctance to risk the heavy ships that had led to the timidity and poor morale

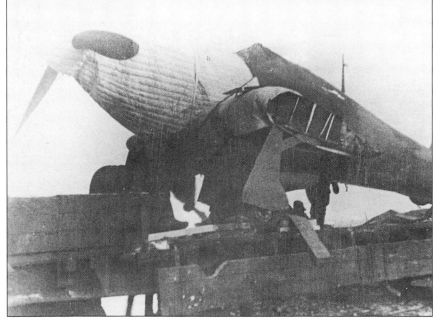

A Soviet light anti-aircraft gun waits for a clear sighting outside of Murmansk. The soldier to the left of the gun is using a range finder to determine the distance to the target.

During the early years of the war Great Britain supplied hundreds of aircraft to the USSR via the Arctic ports. Here, a Hurricane fighter is being loaded for transport to points south.

of the Kriegsmarine in Norway. Raeder produced a memorandum on the role of the German Navy on 15 January 1943. He pointed out that only a balanced fleet including capital ships could tie down the Royal Navy to any degree and prevent it from concentrating its whole strength against the U-boats. Basing the fleet in Norway forced the British to secure the Atlantic convoy route and equip the Home Fleet with the most modern battleships and several aircraft carriers that could be better used elsewhere. [37]

It was to no avail, though, and Raeder resigned on 30 January. Hitler replaced him with Karl Dönitz. Dönitz prepared a scheme to decommission most of the navy's heavy ships. However, he had no intention of following through such a plan and persuaded Hitler to allow him to use the *Scharnhorst* and *Tirpitz* against the convoys without crippling restrictions.[38] As a result, the repaired and reprieved *Scharnhorst* sailed to Norway in March 1943 to join the *Tirpitz* and *Lützow*, and they then all sailed to Altenfjord in the extreme north of Norway.

An interesting alternative use of the PTRD 14.5mm anti-tank rifle was as an anti-aircraft gun. This single shot weapon could, in the hands of a crack-shot, deliver a fatal blow to slow, lightly protected reconnaissance aircraft. This gun is part of the Soviet defences around Murmansk.

The whole strategic position hung on the *Tirpitz*. There remained no real defence against her if she sortied against an Arctic convoy in earnest. The British had made numerous bombing attempts against the *Tirpitz* in her anchorage in Trondheim, and in October 1942 a joint Special Operations Executive (SOE)/Royal Navy midget submarine attack had been aborted remarkably close to the target. Since the *Tirpitz*'s move to Altenfjord put it beyond the range of RAF aircraft, the Royal Navy decided to try again, this time using three-man X-Craft submarines. Six of these midget submarines were towed across the North Sea by T and S Class submarines of the Home Flotillas. By 20 September they were in position outside Altenfjord, although only

four were able to make the attack, as *X-8* was scuttled and *X-9* was lost with all her crew. The X-Craft reached their objective on 22 September. Two of the craft, *X-6*, commanded by Lieutenant Donald Cameron, RNR, and *X-7*, commanded by Lieutenant Godfrey Place, RN, managed to negotiate the *Tirpitz's* defences and place their charges beneath her. Cameron and his crew were captured, though Place and one of his crew escaped when attacked by the Germans. Cameron and his crew were taken aboard the target and, "prior to the explosion it is reported that the crew of *X-6* were seen looking anxiously at their watches." At least two charges went off at 08:30 hours and "the *Tirpitz* was heaved five or six feet [1.5 – 1.8m] out the water." The surviving British crews were "well treated and given hot coffee and schnapps." Indeed, the German sailors "expressed great admiration of their bravery."[39] Both Place and Cameron were awarded the Victoria Cross.

The German battleship had been seriously damaged. The 2032-tonne (2000-ton) "C" turret had been lifted by the explosion and then dropped down and jammed.

Allied merchant ships under attack during the Battle of the Barents Sea. The engagement was an humiliating defeat for the Kriegsmarine.

Admiral Kummetz was fortunately on leave when the Scharnhorst *sailed to intercept a convoy in December 1943. He would otherwise have commanded the task force that lost one of Germany's best warships.*

One of the turbines had been shaken from its bed, and much damage had been done to range finders and the fire control systems. The turret could not be repaired without a visit to a German dockyard as no floating crane could lift it. The damage to the hull required a dry dock. Dönitz told Hitler of the attack on 24 September and, as he feared for the ship's safety on a journey to Germany, they agreed she should remain in Norway and have repairs made in situ. However, Dönitz, "considered that the ship might never again regain complete operational efficiency."[40] They hoped to have the major repairs completed by the middle of March 1944. In addition to this, the *Lützow* sailed from Norway for the Baltic on 26 September. The Kriegsmarine's strength in Norway was now very much weaker.

THE SINKING OF THE *SCHARNHORST*

This reduction in German forces and the return of the British Home Fleet to something like full strength after the invasion of Sicily in July 1943 enabled the British to take a more offensive stance off the coast of Norway, and also restart the convoys. A carrier-launched air attack took place against the port of Bodo in early October, and the first convoys in nine months, JW54A and B, safely reached the Kola inlet by late November. RA54A also returned without incident.

In December the next convoy, JW55A, sailed. It arrived safely although it was spotted by German reconnaissance aircraft. Admiral Dönitz finally secured from Hitler the authority to commit his remaining heavy surface units against the Arctic convoys in early 1943. However, given the cessation of the convoys in the summer, there had been little opportunity and the Kriegsmarine in Norway had been somewhat inactive. Thus the German naval staff issued orders in November stating that "the functions of the ships remain unaltered . . . Against this Traffic [the Arctic convoys] both the Northern Task Force [essentially the *Scharnhorst* and the destroyers] and the U-boats are to be employed." Admiral Kummetz, the task force commander, preferred to wait for the completion of the *Tirpitz*'s repairs and restrict himself to forays with the destroyers. However, Dönitz gained Hitler's permission to commit the battle cruiser against the next convoy on 19 December 1943. He also reinforced the two U-boat flotillas in Norway.[41] With Kummetz on leave, Rear-Admiral Bey, commanding the destroyers, was given the task of attacking the convoy.

On 20 December JW55B sailed from Loch Awe. As well as the normal comple-
ment of destroyers, cover was provided by three cruisers under Vice-Admiral
Burnett, while distant protection was down to the Commander-in-Chief Home
Fleet, Bruce Fraser, aboard the battleship *Duke of York*. The convoy was spotted by a
German meteorological flight on 22 December. The Luftwaffe rediscovered it on
25 December and soon there was a single U-boat in company, with another seven in
the area. Admiral Schniewind, commander of Group North, tried to have the operation postponed in view of inadequate intelligence, but the extreme pressure of the

The German battleship Scharnhorst *was sunk in December 1943 by British ships during a foray against an Arctic convoy.*

situation on the Eastern Front was pressed upon him and he ordered that the *Scharnhorst* put to sea on 25 December 1943.[42] British Ultra intelligence revealed the fact to the Royal Navy and Fraser was informed of the intelligence in the early hours of the following day.

The heavy seas had forced Admiral Bey to detach his destroyer escort. So he was alone when his ship encountered Burnett's cruisers on the morning of 26 December. The British sighted the German ship first and opened fire at 09:29 hours, disabling her forward radar. The *Scharnhorst* turned away and used her superior speed to break contact. Bey made a further attempt to close on the convoy, but was again intercepted by Burnett's ships two hours later. Meanwhile, Fraser on *Duke of York*, in company with the cruiser *Jamaica* and four destroyers, had placed himself between the *Scharnhorst* and her base at Altenfjord. The *Duke of York* picked her up on radar at 16:17 hours, and as the range closed the *Duke of York* and *Jamaica* were able to open fire at 16:50 hours. The *Scharnhorst* was caught unawares and turned north into the path of Burnett. As the *Scharnhorst* tried to open the distance the battle became a gunfire duel between the two capital ships. Hits from the *Duke of York* slowed the German ship and her firing stopped. The British destroyers then attacked and torpedo hits sealed the *Scharnhorst*'s fate by slowing her further. By 19:30 hours her speed was down to five knots and Fraser sent in the destroyers and cruisers to finish her off with torpedoes.[43] It is not known when the *Scharnhorst* sank, probably it was about 19:45 hours. Of her crew of 1903 and 40 cadets only 36 were saved.

The sinking of the *Scharnhorst* was an important British victory. The superiority of British radar, their intelligence provided by Ultra, and Fraser and Burnett's handling of their ships had removed the threat of the last enemy capital ship operational in Norway. German mistakes had contributed to the defeat, too. The Luftwaffe had cooperated poorly with the navy: a seaplane had spotted the British ships but there had been no swift relay of the information to Bey. Bey himself was inexperienced in capital ship operations as he said himself when

Survivors of the Scharnhorst *on the catapult deck of HMS* Duke of York, *one of the Royal Navy ships that sank the German ship.*

A victorious homecoming: the battleship Duke of York *in British home waters after her heroics against the* Scharnhorst.

appointed Kummetz's stand-in: "the last time I was aboard a capital ship was as a cadet."[44] The German Navy had been desperate to justify itself, had put to sea in unfavourable conditions and consequently had been caught by the British. Now with the *Scharnhorst* gone, the *Tirpitz* immobilized and the *Lützow* returned to Germany, the most serious menace to the convoys had gone. It was a turning point in the naval war around Norway. From 1941 to the end of 1943, the Royal Navy had been on the defensive, protecting the convoys and ensuring the German surface forces did not break out into the Atlantic Ocean. With the changed situation the British could go on the offensive, even using the tactically defensive convoys to a strategically aggressive end. Once won, the British never lost the initiative that the Germans had taken from them in April and May 1940. By the end of 1943, therefore, the German Navy in Norway was to all intents and purposes beaten.

The removal of the threat of the two German capital ships ended any serious notion of a balanced German fleet. The U-boats remained a potent weapon, but they would never be able to overwhelm and destroy totally an escorted convoy. German air resources in northern Norway were largely limited to reconnaissance aircraft. Yet the *Tirpitz*, sitting in its anchorage at Altenfjord, might still become a threat once more. Repairs were proceeding apace and there was no intention of sending her south. In January Dönitz even suggested reinforcing her with the *Prinz Eugen*, then in the Baltic.[45] So the Germans might well use her against the convoys although she was not fully operational. Thus as her repairs neared completion, the Royal Navy took matters into its own hands, being unable to persuade RAF Bomber Command to attack the German battleship. Gaining complete tactical surprise on the morning of 3 April 1944, Royal Naval carrier-borne Barracudas achieved 14 hits on the *Tirpitz*, and although none of the damage was very serious, the ship was put out of action for a further three months. Dönitz was determined that fresh repairs be made, as he was well aware of the Royal Navy resources she tied down. [46]

END GAME

With the *Tirpitz* damaged, the Royal Navy became increasing aggressive off the Norwegian coast. As the Arctic convoys had been halted to release shipping for Operation Overlord, the Allied invasion of Normandy, the Royal Navy attempted to harass Norwegian coastal traffic and simulate a threat to Norway as part of the deception plan "Fortitude North". It was hoped that these operations would encourage the Germans to keep their large U-boat forces in the area rather than use them against the shipping supplying Allied forces in Normandy. Once the success of Overlord began to release destroyers for other missions, the British Admiralty considered restarting the Arctic convoys. It was conceivable that a repaired *Tirpitz* might be capable of limited operations against them, though. Further carrier-borne air strikes showed that whoever was protecting the ship had "learnt his lessons", as formidable defences now were in place.[47] The main problem was that Fleet Air Arm aircraft could not carry a bomb heavy enough to damage seriously the ship. So the RAF was the only alternative. Plans were laid, and on 15 September 1944 RAF Lancasters flying out of Yagodnik airfield in Russia carrying 12,000lb Tall Boy bombs attacked the *Tirpitz* at anchor. They

The German battleship
Tirpitz *had a major*
influence on naval
operations in the Arctic
theatre, even though she
never saw any naval action
in the Atlantic Ocean.

achieved a single direct hit, which was enough to blow a hole in her forward deck on the starboard side. The battleship was lucky to still be afloat.[48]

The Red Army launched an offensive in the far north in June 1944, which forced Finland to seek terms (see Chapter 6). The Finnish-Soviet armistice of 19 September made the German position in northern Norway extremely precarious, as the Soviet advance carried the Red Army into Norwegian Finnmark. At a meeting on 20 September, Dönitz and the Naval War Staff concluded that, "it was no longer possible to make the *Tirpitz* ready for sea and action again." Rather than risk towing her back to Germany, they decided to move the ship to Tromso for use as a floating battery against any British landing. Hitler still believed this a possibility in late 1944, although Dönitz remained sceptical.[49] The *Tirpitz* moved to her new berth at Tromso on 15 October. The Germans rested the only partially seaworthy battleship on a sandbank and surrounded her with anti-aircraft defences and a double net barrage brought down from Altenfjord. However, the move to Tromso sealed the battleship's fate. Whatever the man-made defences there was no protective mountain above the ship as there had been at Trondheim and Altenfjord. More importantly, she was now within range of RAF bombers based in Great Britain. She was attacked on 28 October and again on 12 November. At 09:40 hours on

The rail network in Russia was the most reliable form of all-weather transport, particularly in the remote Arctic region. The Soviet officer seated right and his companion are members of a line of communications formation.

The stability of the Arctic Front made the erection of substantial buildings such as these worthwhile, as well as necessary given the weather. A plentiful supply of timber for building was readily available. These are Russian lodgings outside Murmansk.

12 November, the *Tirpitz*'s main armament opened up on the incoming Lancasters. The ship's captain, Weber, frantically requested air cover from Bardufoss airfield, to no avail. *Tirpitz* was hit twice and then capsized. About 1000 of her crew were trapped inside her, only 85 could be rescued by cutting through the hull.

The *Tirpitz* had been based in Norway for three years, and while she achieved nothing in action, her mere presence caused the Royal Navy inordinate problems. The possibility of her attacking the Arctic convoys, or breaking into the Atlantic, had had a disproportionate effect on British naval strategy. The Home Fleet was constantly kept up to strength with modern battleships and aircraft carriers that could have been better used elsewhere, but for the threat of the *Tirpitz*. The Royal Navy had risked and lost valuable cruisers in the Barents Sea, been forced to cancel convoys, and had scattered PQ17 due to the possibility of the battleship attacking. Thus the Royal Navy and RAF had expended considerable time, effort and lives to remove the danger she posed.

With the removal of this threat, and the almost total lack of German bomber aircraft in Norway, the Royal Navy was able to dominate the Norwegian coast. The disruption of iron ore traffic was a useful strategic goal. More important were the Arctic convoys. When the Royal Navy gained the upper hand in the Battle of the Atlantic in mid-1943, it shifted to offensive anti-U-boat operations. Within two months, U-boat command suspended pack operations in the Atlantic. With the *Scharnhorst* sunk, the *Tirpitz* crippled, and the Luftwaffe presence in northern Norway much reduced, the U-boats remained the principal threat to the Arctic convoys. Dönitz intended to wait until the introduction of the new Type XXI U-boats before restarting the Atlantic campaign. However, the worsening situation on the Eastern Front and the perceived need to stop the Arctic convoys led the Kriegsmarine to regard attacks on the convoys as an essentially defensive commitment. Dönitz therefore increased the number of U-boats in Norway to 33 by moving 20 Atlantic boats there in January 1945, in response to the British restarting the convoys that month.

THE ARCTIC CONVOYS IN RETROSPECT

The historiography of the Arctic convoys has usually emphasized their defensive nature. This was certainly true of the period 1941–43 when the Soviet Union was in serious need of the supplies. However, out of the over 1,000,000 tonnes (984,000 tons) of supplies transported to Russia by the convoys in 1944–45, much of it remained unused. Naval historian Andrew Lambert has argued that rather than the traditional view that the "safe and timely arrival" was the key to the Arctic convoys after February 1944, "the critical factor in the Arctic was the ability to inflict casualties on the enemy."[50] The convoys were never critical to British survival, and when more important British interests were at stake they were suspended. However, the destruction of the German U-boat arm remained a vital strategic goal. Thus the Royal Navy created a battle of attrition in the Arctic that the Germans were forced to fight.

The Arctic was the only area where the U-boats remained in large concentrations. Success in the Atlantic allowed the British to shift experienced anti-submarine warfare forces to the Arctic convoy route. The Home Fleet was prepared to commit two or three escort carriers, and the British were reading Enigma almost as fast as it was sent. The convoys were basically "fought through" to their destination. During the second half of 1944, 159 ships left for Russia, and all arrived safely; 100 set out for home, and only two were lost. The Germans lost nine U-boats. In 1945, the Germans switched tactics, congregating in the Kola inlet rather than forming a patrol line off Bear Island.

Royal Navy operations in Norwegian waters had also led to the stationing of increased numbers of Luftwaffe torpedo bombers in the north. Consequently, the convoys during the last six months of the war met with remarkably stiff

The Tirpitz *was heavily protected by anti-aircraft guns and, as can be seen here, anti-submarine nets.*

resistance. Heavy air attacks were launched against JW64 and RA64 and were beaten off with serious Luftwaffe losses. Despite schnorkel-equipped U-boats and a tightening of U-boat signals and the resultant loss of Ultra, U-boat losses were high. In 1944–45, there were 11 round-trip Arctic convoys. In 1943, convoy escorts had not sunk any U-boats. In 1944–45, they sunk 21, and shore-based aircraft a further four. This was 25 U-boats out of a total of 32 sunk on all Arctic convoys. The increased offensive effort resulted in higher losses for the escorts, though. Before 1944 the U-boats had sunk one escort, in 1944 they sunk three, and in 1945 a further four. There were also higher mercantile losses, too: no merchantmen were lost in 1943, 11 thereafter.[51] This must be judged a reasonable and economic price, though.

The RAF also conducted bombing raids against the U-boat pens at Bergen and Trondheim because the Admiralty was fearful of a new U-boat offensive by superior Type XXI and Type XXIII submarines. Occasionally they were lucky: in October 1944, catching four U-boats moored in the open. However, even 12,000lb Tall Boy bombs failed to penetrate the 3.9m (13ft) roof of the Bergen pens. It is difficult to judge the effects of these RAF attacks on the U-boat bases in Norway. Had the war continued, and a second U-boat offensive developed using new submarines and technology, the Norwegian bases might have become of crucial importance. However, the Germans never regained the initiative, and with production dislocated by constant RAF and United States Army Air Force (USAAF) bombing, the feared Type XXI did not enter service until April 1945, far too late to affect the outcome of the war.

The last wartime Arctic convoy, JW66, sailed on 16 April 1945 and arrived safely without encountering the enemy. The return convoy, RA66, left Kola on 29 April. A preliminary sweep of the inlet accounted for two U-boats, and in the last contact of the war, the frigate HMS *Goodall* was sunk by Lieutenant Westphalen in *U-968*. The Arctic naval war was over.

CONCLUSION

Norway was of vital importance to Germany in the war at sea. German naval thinking had recognized this since World War I, and *Weserübung* was essentially a Kriegsmarine victory. Although Norway's strategic importance diminished with the fall of France in 1940, Great Britain's decision to supply the Soviet Union by the Arctic route changed that, as Hitler decided to send his heavy surface units to Norway. German possession of the country gave its forces a whole

British Barracudas on their way to attack the Tirpitz *in April 1944. The attacks put the battleship out of action for a further three months.*

host of advantages in the convoy battles. Norway sat on the southern flank of a convoy route where the Germans set up a series of excellent sea and air bases, most out of range or invulnerable to British land-based bombing for the first years of the war.

Once the Germans decided to make a serious effort against the convoys, a pattern became clear. The experience of the early convoys of 1942 showed that the ships could be fought through against the U-boats and German aircraft, although often with serious losses, if good convoy discipline was maintained. The *Tirpitz* and other heavy units changed all that. One or more of these ships could overwhelm the destroyer and cruiser escort and thus annihilate the convoy. This was spectacularly demonstrated by the scattering of PQ17 caused by the mere possibility of the sailing of the *Tirpitz*. The lengths the British went to sink the *Tirpitz* are therefore hardly surprising. Her presence alone forced them to keep battleships and aircraft carriers in the Home Fleet.

A WAR OF ATTRITION

Yet even once their heavy units were sunk or crippled, the Germans still had to attack the convoys. They perceived a direct link between the Allied supplies getting through and the progress of the war on the Eastern Front. As Dönitz put it, "in view of the bitter fighting on the Eastern Front I feel it is my duty to deploy these ships [the *Scharnhorst* and *Tirpitz*]."[52] Similarly, German naval historians calculate that the 500,000 vehicles that arrived in Murmansk between August 1944 and April 1945 were vital and enabled the Soviets to equip some 60 additional motorized divisions. To quote Vice-Admiral Friedrich Ruge: "Thus Anglo-American sea power also exerted decisive influence on land operations in Eastern Europe."[53] So even in 1945 the Germans had to send their limited resources out against the convoys and fight a battle of attrition that was to the Royal Navy's advantage.

The Royal Navy reckoned that had the positions been reversed they would have destroyed every Arctic convoy.[54] Indeed, considering the resources available to the Germans in surface craft, submarines and aircraft, it is almost inexplicable they did not cause the British far worse problems in the Arctic. The indecisive use of the Kriegsmarine was due to poor leadership from Hitler downwards. The Führer placed crippling limits on his major surface units and had no sound concept of their use. His hesitancy sapped morale and created a cautious attitude. When the ships were used, their commanders showed considerable timidity, as at the Battle of the Barents Sea (see above), or incompetence, such as when the *Scharnhorst* was sunk. Raeder had prophesied on 3 September 1939 that his "surface forces . . . can do no more than show they know how to die gallantly", and die gallantly they did in their thousands aboard the *Scharnhorst* and *Tirpitz*. It was a sacrifice in vain, though.

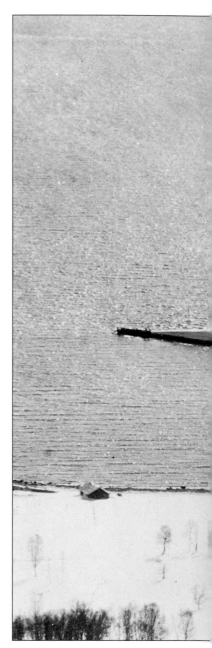

The wreck of the Tirpitz *at Tromso, November 1944. Nearly 1000 of her crew died when she capsized.*

Chapter 6

RED STORM —
STALIN'S
REVENGE

The 1944 Soviet summer offensive broke like a thunderstorm on the Finnish Front. After three years of relative inactivity, the Red Army tore into German and Finnish forces and rolled them back, knocking Finland out of the war.

The Finns and Germans on the Arctic and Karelian Fronts had grown dangerously accustomed to a quiet life while their colleagues farther south were dealt one deadly blow after another by a resurgent and battle-hardened Red Army. By the summer of 1944, the time had come for Stalin to settle scores in the north.

Stalingrad was the end of the beginning for the USSR, and the beginning of the end for Hitler. After this battle nothing would be the same. In January 1943 – the same month as the German defeat at Stalingrad – the Red Army restored contact with Leningrad by opening a narrow corridor between the Volkhov and

The anti-tank rifle platoon of a Soviet infantry regiment arrives at a newly established battalion headquarters near the Norwegian border. Many of the soldiers are wearing the pilotka *forage cap.*

Neva Rivers. The fall of Leningrad would seal Finland's fate, as the entire Finno-German front from the Baltic Sea to the Arctic Ocean began to unravel.

For the Finns the question was when and how, rather than if, they were to pull out of the war. They were determined to save their Motherland, even if it meant securing some kind of peace with Stalin and risking a war with Hitler. On 5 March 1943, a new government with a more pro-Allied outlook was appointed. When the new Finnish foreign minister, Ramsay, visited Berlin he refused to be browbeaten by von Ribbentrop into signing a mutual declaration that neither of the allies would make a separate peace with Stalin. An infuriated Hitler recalled his Helsinki ambassador.[1]

The Germans had realized for some time that retaining Finland as an ally depended upon the German Army maintaining its stranglehold on Leningrad, or even capturing it. Earlier German plans to storm Leningrad were shelved.[2] The German defeat at Kursk in July 1943 ended these plans permanently. By the end of that month the Red Army made a probing attack against Army Group North and Küchler, its commander, made preparations to fall back some 200km (125 miles) to the Panther Line at Narva.[3]

Hitler knew Finland, his "loyal" ally, had made approaches to Moscow but had rejected Stalin's demands. To show his displeasure, Hitler called in the Finnish ambassador and gave the hapless diplomat the verbal abuse the Führer usually reserved for unsatisfactory subordinates.[4]

Soviet infantry cross a river on the back of a T-34 tank at the beginning of the Soviet offensive. In the foreground is a German gun which has had its breech blown out to prevent its use by Red Army gunners.

On 17 January 1944 the Red Army broke out of its Oranienbaum bridgehead and also advanced to the east of Leningrad. Küchler ordered Army Group North to retreat to the Panther Line on 30 January. By 12 February the Russians were approaching Narva, and Paasakivi was sent to Stockholm to sound out what terms Stalin was willing to give Finland for a separate peace. He flew to Moscow but negotiations proved pointless. Stalin's demands were too harsh. In the meantime Marshal Model, who had replaced Küchler as commander of Army Group North, had stabilized the front along the Panther Line. The German occupation of another wavering ally, Hungary, in March 1944 served as a dire warning to the Finns of what happened to "traitors". As another warning, Hitler suspended deliveries of vitally needed foodstuffs and arms shipments to Finland. He also laid careful plans to deal with Finland should it attempt to change sides. On 16 February 1944, Hitler ordered preparations to carry out Operation Tanne: the occupation of Aland (Tanne West) and Suursaari (Tanne East). Aland was to be occupied by the 416th Infantry Division and one parachute regiment, while Model's forces were to occupy Suursaari. In the Arctic, Operation Birke was prepared: the German mountain troops were to abandon their forward positions in Soviet Lapland and Finland. They were then to retreat to a prepared position at Ivalo and along the Pasvik River, where they were to cover Petsamo and the Kolosjoki nickel mines. It was, believed Hitler, imperative to defend these mines at all cost and a further retreat into Norway was not contemplated.[5]

RAW MATERIALS – THE KEY FACTOR

The Kolosjoki (Nikel)[6] mining area was heavily defended by a strong garrison and the heaviest anti-aircraft defences on the Eastern Front, while the nearby hydro-electrical power plant of Jäniskoski had been covered by a massive concrete cap against Soviet and Allied bombing raids.[7] The mine, however, proved a miserable failure. The Germans had hoped that production would reach 10,160 tonnes (10,000 tons) per year by the end of 1941. In February 1943 it was still only producing half that amount. Göring, as head of German industrial production, intervened and with Albert Speer, the young and ruthless armaments minister, got production increased. In a period of 20 months some 394,208 tonnes (388,000 tons) were produced. In August 1944, Speer reported to Hitler that stocks in Germany would last until June 1946. There was no need, therefore, to defend the mines.[8] Hitler had no reason to object to a complete withdrawal from the region east of Pasvik, and this would serve to save the Lapland Army (now renamed Twentieth Mountain Army) from the clutches of the Red Army when it attacked.

On 1 May, Stalin decided that the Red Army would first deal with the Finns and make them accept his "peace" terms: ceding back Karelia, leasing another base area, handing over the Petsamo Corridor and paying a huge indemnity (of £150,000,000) to the USSR. Stalin, realizing the Finns had to be defeated first before they would accept his bitter pills, chose to concentrate 450,000 troops, 800 tanks, 2000 aircraft and 10,000 artillery guns in four massive armies along the Finnish Front. These armies were the Thirty-Second at Maselskaya, General Meretskov's Seventh Army along the Svir and on the Isthmus, General Cherepanov's Twenty-Third Army and General Govorov's Twenty-First. By comparison, the Finnish Army had 270,000 troops, 110 tanks (light and obsolete), 248 aircraft and 1900 guns. It had no modern weapons to defeat Soviet T-34 tanks or Sturmovik ground-attack aircraft. After more than two years of trench warfare the Finnish troops were unfit to deal with the new, Blitzkrieg-style of Soviet warfare. The Finnish High Command had neglected their fixed defences as well, and it was only in March 1944 that these began to be upgraded. It was all too little, too late. By June the main defence line on the Isthmus, the VT Line, would still be unable to withstand a Russian attack. Mannerheim made the situation far worse by making two disastrous decisions. He committed the bulk of his forces to Karelia and decided to hold eastern (Russian) Karelia as a bargaining chip in future "talks" with Moscow. He also did not believe Stalin was in earnest about an offensive against Finland. He thought it was only a bluff to get Finland to negotiate a withdrawal from the war and that if, against all expectations, Stalin did attack, then his troops would strike Karelia first and not the Isthmus. Mannerheim's strategic and political delusions account for much of the

Carefully working their way through the rubble, a Soviet team presses hard on the Germans' heels in June 1944. In the centre of the group is a flamethrower operator with an ROKS-2 weapon.

Obviously the cameraman had a good head for heights. The Soviet heavy field gun is an ML-20 152mm piece raised to almost maximum elevation. In Stalin's words: "Artillery is the God of War".

Finnish Army's near disastrous performance during the initial stages of the Soviet offensive.[9]

On 9 June, the Russians attacked General Laatikainen's IV Corps with 500 dive-bombers and a gigantic artillery barrage from 800 rocket launchers and some 5500 artillery pieces. This deadly performance was repeated the day after when XXX Guards Army Corps attacked the Finnish 10th Division and immediately broke through. When the Finns found their anti-tank guns to be no more effective than pop guns their morale collapsed, and one regiment fled in panic to the rear. The 10th Division, losing its artillery, ceased to function as a proper fighting unit. Mannerheim was forced to order a general retreat to the VT Line that same afternoon.

The marshal ordered reinforcements from Karelia (of one division and one brigade). He placed the Armoured Division behind the 11th Division, which now covered its own and the 10th Division's front with only nine battalions thinly spread along their extended front. On 14 June a Soviet division, supported by one tank brigade, attacked a single Finnish infantry company at Kuuterselkä where the Finns had not expected the Russians to strike. XXX Guards Army Corps poured through the breach, overrunning both the Finnish Cavalry Brigade and the Armoured Division. The Finns lost a third of their troops, and were only saved from being encircled by the Soviet corps' single-minded drive towards Viipuri. The Finns fell back to their second line of defence – the VKT Line – and on 18 June Mannerheim requested German assistance. The German response was both swift and generous. The 122nd Division was ordered to cross the Gulf of Finland, anti-tanks guns were dispatched across that same stretch of water in torpedo boats, while 70 Stukas were dispatched to put some beef into the Finnish Air Force. Hitler's only demand was that the Finns were to hold the VKT Line.

By 20 June that seemed like an impossible task. Viipuri was held by the 20th Brigade, which lacked morale and combat experience in equal measure. When Russian tanks appeared on the city's outskirts during the early morning, the Finnish artillery quickly ran short of ammunition. Later in the afternoon, when the brigade's commander ordered his HQ to the rear, this was taken by the jittery troops as a signal for a general retreat – the whole brigade fled from its positions. Viipuri, defended so heroically back in 1940, fell with hardly a whimper on 20 June four years later.

THE FINNS BEGIN TO WAVER

The Finnish public was shocked by their army's poor showing and it dented both their, and German, confidence in the Finnish Army's ability to stave off the Russians. In Helsinki, late June proved to be a dramatic interlude in the fighting. President Ryti wanted to open negotiations with the Russians but found himself the reluctant host to von Ribbentrop, who appeared in Helsinki uninvited on 22 June. Von Ribbentrop wanted a pledge by the Finns to fight to the bitter end. Mannerheim pointed out that the Finns desperately needed German support and persuaded Ryti to sign. Although von Ribbentrop smelt a rat, he decided to accept their assurances. On 26 June von Ribbentrop departed from Helsinki, little knowing that the Finns had no intention whatsoever of being tied to Ryti's pledge.

Five days earlier the Soviet Stavka had given its armies new orders. General Korobnikov's Fifty-Ninth Army was to cross from the Narva Front, land outside Vyborg, outflank the VKT Line and repeat Timoshenko's offensive during the Winter War. The Twenty-First Army was to break through the VKT line at Tali, link up with Korobnikov and advance to the Kymi River, while the Twenty-Third Army was to cross the Vuoksi River at Vuosalmi and march to Lake Ladoga. The Seventh and Thirty-Second Armies, led by Meretskov, would then attack the Finnish Army in Karelia. Thus Finland was to be defeated and the Red Army troops, desperately needed against the Germans, would be shifted north and southwards.

The front commanders acted immediately upon Stavka orders, and on 25 June XXX Guards Corps attacked Tali held by the Finnish 17th Division, which gave way immediately. But the Armoured Division, supported by the newly arrived and tough German Assault Gun Brigade, put up fierce resistance to the Russian advance. Attacks by the Russians from 30 June to 6 July did not achieve a breakthrough. The Fifty-Ninth Army landed on the coast on 1 July, when fighting around Tali was definitely

Sniping called for patience, good eyesight and a cool head. This Russian sniper is armed with a Mosin Nagant Model 91/30 equipped with a PU sniper sight. Priority targets for snipers were enemy officers and NCOs.

going in the Finns' favour. It was only on 7 July that Korobnikov's forces attacked the mainland, but this time the Russians faced not only the Finnish 10th Division and Cavalry Brigade (both rested and refitted) but also the German 122nd Division. The Finno-German forces put up a fierce resistance until 9 July, when Korobnikov admitted he could not establish a bridgehead and broke off the offensive.

But that same day, the Twenty-Third Army crossed the Vuoksi with two divisions and expanded its bridgehead on the northern side of the river very slowly. The Russians were even more exhausted than the Finns, and Stavka had already ordered a halt to their offensive on 11 July. Why had the Red Army, so swift in its advance and confident of victory in early June, run out of steam? One reason was that the Finns had restored their forces to good discipline and order. They had received modern German equipment and military personnel; the Stukas had also proved effective against the long and densely packed Russian columns;[10] while the German *panzerfausts* (anti-tank rockets) had taken a deadly toll among the Russian T-34s. Most of all, the Russians had underestimated the Finns and their formidable terrain once again, and had failed to coordinate their attacks properly.

In Karelia, too, the Russian plans had not come to fruition. Meretskov had two armies, with 15 rifle divisions, 3 marine brigades, 1 armoured brigade and 1 artillery assault corps at his disposal. The Finnish Karelian Army had been weakened by

Mannerheim's transfer of three divisions to shore up the Isthmus Front, so it seemed that Meretskov could make mincemeat of the Finns. But Mannerheim had anticipated Meretskov's move on 16 June by ordering a swift retreat to the U Line just east of the 1940 border. The retreat was orderly and unhurried (in stark contrast to developments on the Isthmus) when the Russians began their offensive on 21 June. Two days later, the Russians landed marines behind the Finnish lines on the Ladoga shore and cut the main rail line. They established a bridgehead which the Finns could not, despite repeated attacks, either dislodge or reduce in size. The Finns chose to bypass it and continue their retreat westwards.

The Thirty-Second Army that had struck along the Svir encountered even weaker resistance than the Seventh Army farther north. The Finnish troops deserted and fled in panic at the sight of the Russian tanks and massed infantry. But here their commanders very quickly restored discipline, and managed to get almost all their troops safely back to the U Line. The retreat ended on 28 July and the Finns prepared themselves for the inevitable Russian onslaught.

Stavka was deeply disappointed that no Finnish troops had been captured, and chose to despatch CXXVII Light Corps to the front to speed up Meretskov's advance. When this too failed to get things going, it reprimanded the general for his slow and clumsy advance. Mannerheim had in the meantime reinforced the Karelian Army with troops transferred from the Isthmus, so that when the Russians did attack,

The difficulties of moving even small field guns like this on the Finnish Front are apparent. The gun is the standard Red Army divisional weapon, a 76mm ZiS-3, which could be used as either a field gun or in the anti-tank role.

Peering through the tree tops is the barrel of an ML20 152 heavy field gun. The Red Army prided itself on the efficiency of its artillery, a tradition that dated back to the early years of the nineteenth century.

between 10 and 17 July, they could not break through. On 21 July Meretskov had the satisfaction of knowing that his forces had reached the 1940 border north of Ilomantsi, but his sense of achievement soon turned sour. General Raappana led a vigorous Finnish counterattack that trapped two Soviet divisions, which were broken up, while Soviet relief attacks were also beaten back. During 6–8 August the remaining Russians managed to escape, but they left behind 3000 dead comrades and 94 guns. On 29 August Stavka ended all Soviet offensives against Finland.

This stalemate at the front enabled the Finns to make some crucial changes, and begin disentangling themselves from Hitler without falling entirely into Stalin's grasp. On 4 August Mannerheim was made president of Finland (as well as commander-in-chief) and he immediately made it clear to the Germans that he would not honour Ryti's pledge of support. On 25 August contact was made with Moscow, and a truce was signed on 4 September. De facto peace with the Soviets had been established, but would it lead to war with Germany? Only time would tell.[11]

The Finnish-Soviet truce left the Germans in a potentially disastrous situation, as the Finnish defection would lead to their entire front unravelling. The Twentieth Mountain Army was committed to holding the Petsamo–Pasvik Line in the far north, but would it be able to do so? On 3 September Hitler decided to drop Tanne West for the sake of good relations with Sweden, which had a paramount interest in Aland[12] due to its proximity to Stockholm and its Swedish-speaking population.[13]

The day before, the German Legation in Helsinki was informed that Finland was most reluctantly breaking off diplomatic relations with Nazi Germany forthwith. This did not come unexpectedly since the Germans had feared such a move for months. Nevertheless, it was a serious blow and would entirely undermine the security of the German Lapland Army's southern flank. What made the situation much worse for both sides was the Finnish pledge to Moscow that all German troops would be expelled or interned by the Finnish armed forces by the end of the month. This was a completely unrealistic deadline as the Finns very well knew.

On 6 September Hitler ordered the launching of Birke: to evacuate and save the two southern corps of the Twentieth Mountain Army. Unfortunately Dietl, who had been popular and appreciated by the Finns especially Mannerheim, was dead,[14] and his replacement, Lieutenant-General Lothar Rendulic,[15] while an experienced and tough commander, was entirely unknown to the Finns. Rendulic was also to prove much more uncompromising and ready to carry out his orders, however ruthless, to the letter.

GERMAN DEFENSIVE PLANS

Rendulic did not trust the Finns. He found their explanation that the Russians would not cross the Finnish 1940 border and invade northern Finland one born either of Finnish naïvety or a ruse to lure his exposed army into a trap. Rendulic was convinced the Russians would invade and that he had to operate as if in enemy territory. At the Salla River and eastwards towards Kandalaksha stood XXXVI Mountain Corps, with the 163rd and 169th Divisions, commanded by General Emil Vogel. Farther south was General Friedrich Hochbaum's XVIII Mountain Corps, which held two widely separate sections of front. At Kestenga stood Division Group *Kreutler* (139th Regiment) with the 6th SS Mountain Division *Nord* as support. The 7th Mountain Division held Ukhta – the southernmost point of the German-held front in northern Karelia or southern Lapland.

Rendulic faced an unenviable situation, since the Russians could not only attack his front in the east but his ex-allies could attack from the south. (Then there was the entirely different but equally threatening situation along the Litsa Front.) Rendulic created two forces to cover the southern front: Battle Group West (at Oulu) and Battle Group East (at Hyrynsalmi).

On 7 September Rendulic was taken completely by surprise when the Russians attacked at Korya with infantry and T-34s, which opened the way to Salla, which was captured a few days later. The Germans had thought this area was impassable for tanks and the appearance of these steel monsters had a debilitating effect upon troop morale. XXXVI Mountain Corps abandoned its position along the Verman Line (held since late 1941), and the Russians cut the Salla road on 11 September. Fortunately the Germans had built a more southerly road, and by 14 September the last troops had passed Allakurtti on their way west. General Vogel decided to send

The offensive that knocked Finland out of World War II. The Soviet attack was methodical and remorseless.

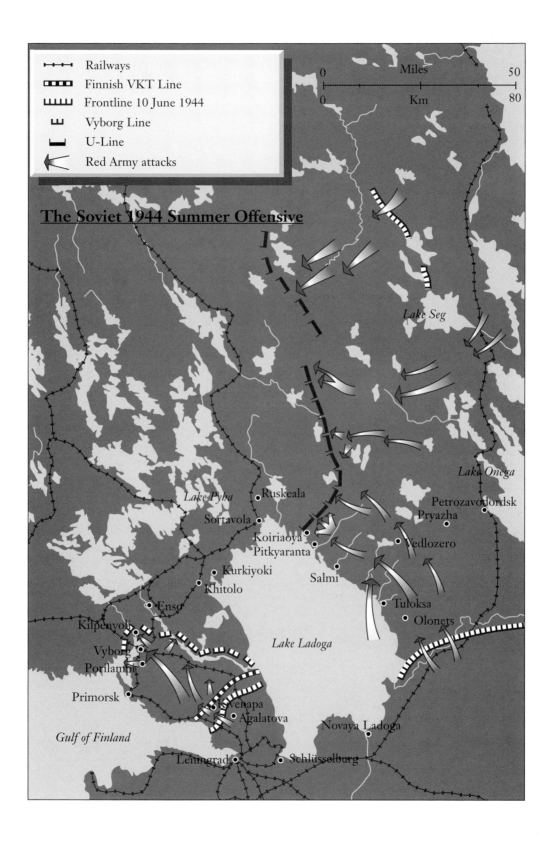

Railways
Finnish VKT Line
Frontline 10 June 1944
Vyborg Line
U-Line
Red Army attacks

The Soviet 1944 Summer Offensive

Miles
0   50
Km
0   80

Lake Seg

Lake Onega

Lake Pyha
Ruskeala
Sortavola
Koiriaoya
Pitkyaranta
Petrozavodordsk
Pryazha
Vedlozero
Salmi
Kurkiyoki
Khitolo
Enso
Tuloksa
Olonets
Kilpenyoli
Vyborg
Porilampi
Lake Ladoga
Primorsk
Isvenapa
Agalatova
Novaya Ladoga
Gulf of Finland
Leningrad
Schlüsselburg

the 169th Division northwards to protect the Arctic Highway between Ivalo and Rovaniemi. Rendulic ordered him to cover XVIII Mountain Corps' retreat northwards through Salla by holding Kayrala and Korya for 10 days. By 24 September the corps had evacuated its positions and retreated towards Rovaniemi through Salla. The Russian pursuit ended at Salla, to the surprise of the Germans. XVIII Mountain Corps had managed to retreat in good order to the Finnish border by mid-September, pursued by four Soviet divisions. In southern Finland all German units had been evacuated by 13 September.

It was just as well, since on 14 September the Germans had tried to carry out Tanne East with 2500 troops, of whom 700 were captured. This humiliating setback was not designed to make the Germans any more positive about their "deserting" ally, and less likely to carry out Birke in a peaceful fashion. That had proceeded in an orderly fashion until Mannerheim realized he had to use tougher methods to get rid of the Germans. He appointed his best general, Siilasvuo, as commander of the Finnish Northern Army and gave him the Armoured Division, three infantry divisions and two independent brigades to push out Rendulic's forces. Siilasvuo flew to Oulu where he drew up a bold, aggressive plan: he would make a landing at the mouth of the Tornio River and thus cut off the retreat of the German XIX Mountain Corps.

He chose not to inform Finnish GHQ (Mikkeli) before the preparations had been made and he argued, like the no-nonsense military man that he was, that if the landing succeeded then GHQ would not grumble.

FINLAND IS SAVED

Siilasvuo's plan came in the nick of time. On 27 September Lieutenant-General Savonenkov (deputy head of the Soviet ACC) arrived at Mikkeli to reject Major-General Airo's previous pussy-footing with the Germans. Unless the Germans were being expelled by force by 08:00 hours on 1 October, Savonenkov promised there would be hell for the Finns to pay. Mannerheim realized Finland's independence (or what was left of it) was on the line. Luckily for him, Siilasvuo's plan was being carried out and at 07:50 hours on 1 October, Colonel Wolfgang Holsti's 11th Infantry Regiment (from the 3rd Division) landed at the mouth of the Tornio River and seized the small port of Röyttä. Finland had been saved by Siilasvuo's bold and dangerous initiative by a mere 10 minutes.

Röyttä lay on a peninsula and was easily defended. It lacked, fortunately for the Finns, a German garrison and the road to Tornio town itself lay open. At the same time Siilasvuo ordered the Finnish 6th Division to attack at Pudasjärvi. The unexpected Finnish assault caught the Germans completely unawares with the loss of almost 80 troops. Rendulic made furious and angry accusations of Finnish treachery to Colonel Willamo, his Finnish liaison officer. Rendulic, who had been ordered by Hitler to carry out a scorched earth policy in Finland and Norway, now had the excuse he needed to carry out his Führer's draconian orders.

Tornio was "held" by 150 German non-combat troops, and the Finns decided to advance on the town immediately. At the same time, General Pajari's 3rd Division advanced south from the bridgehead towards Kemi. But both this advance and Siilasvuo's offensive from the south were held up by the Germans blowing every bridge behind them and putting up stiff resistance.

Rendulic responded swiftly to the Finnish landing at Tornio. Here, he created Battle Group *Tornio* (of one panzer battalion, three infantry battalions and two field artillery battalions), and at Kemi Battle Group *Kemi* under Major-General Kräutler – who had commanded the German forces at Salla and Kestenga. Battle Group *Tornio* was to hold the road from Tornio to Muonio so that XVII Corps could escape into Norway and avoid the Rovaniemi bottleneck. Kräutler's task was to block the advance of Colonel Kuisto's 15th Brigade along the coastal road from Oulu, and hold Kemi at all costs.

The Germans held the initiative until General Kalle Heiskanen's 11th Division arrived by sea from Oulu between 4 and 5 October. On 6 October the 50th Infantry Regiment advanced north, occupied Tornio and pushed north, where the road was cleared by 8 October. But the Germans had managed to escape. Farther inland the 7th Mountain Division (XVII Mountain Corps) put up an excellent defence against the advancing Finnish forces, which allowed the whole of XXXVI Mountain Corps

The German retreat. An abandoned German artillery position looks out across ground that it had dominated for three years. That it should be constructed of wood is unsurprising as the material was so readily to hand.

to escape from its positions at Salla and Kestenga. But there was a high cost to the Finns of this German defence. When the Finns finally reached Rovaniemi, the capital of Finnish Lapland with a pre-war population of 10,000, there was only a handful of houses left standing. The fires had been set off by a burning ammunition train according to the Germans, by deliberate arson according to the contemporary Finnish view. The war in Lapland was turning into a real, savage conflict between real enemies, perhaps made more vicious by their former cooperation.

Stalin had no interest in intervening in northern Finland against the German XVIII and XXXVI Mountain Corps, holding Ukhta and the Salla/Kestenga sectors. He wanted the distasteful task of fighting a former ally that had supported Finland to the hilt undertaken by the Finns themselves. This was Stalin's own special humiliation to the Finns, which no doubt satisfied his lust for revenge and blood against Finland: a nation that had yet again escaped his clutches. But when his own Arctic offensive, as we shall see, did not develop as fast or gained as much territory as he wanted, he would put more pressure on Finland. As yet another affront and challenge to the Finns, Stalin had appointed his ruthless party hack and Leningrad party boss, Andrei Zhdanov, as head of the ACC. Zhdanov was the same man who had been instrumental in getting Stalin to unleash the Winter War.

In a territory so interlaced with waterways, bridge building was a skill honed to perfection. Under the watchful eyes of a group of officers, Red Army engineers work away in an icy stream during the 1944 Soviet offensive.

On 16 October Zhdanov sent an aggressive and threateningly worded note to Mannerheim demanding a more "vigorous" campaign against the Germans. Again Mannerheim, acutely aware of Stalin's threats and what they implied, did not tarry and ordered Siilasvuo to send the 11th Division along the Tornio (border) road while the 3rd Division advanced around the Germans and seized Muonio. This would cut off the German retreat along the border road northwards. The Armoured Division was to advance, spearheaded by the Jäger Brigade, along the Arctic Highway and occupy Ivalo before the Russians (from the Soviet Fourteenth Army) did so. The 6th Division was to take Kemijärvi to cut off the German retreat.

But it was too late, and Rendulic had managed to pull XVII Mountain Corps to the *Sturmbock* Line at Kautokeino and XXVI Mountain Corps to the *Schultzwallstellung* Line south of Ivalo without too much interference from Finnish forces. The Finnish 11th Division's advance was both slow and cautious due to the lack of heavy weaponry, which their determined and well-equipped enemy possessed. The last fighting took place at Muonio and then at Karesuanto on 28 November. The following day the Germans broke off all contact with the Finns. They dug into the *Sturmbock* Line, west of the Lätäseno River, until January 1945. It was only on 25 April 1945 that the Germans pulled out of their last positions

In densely wooded areas such as this it was necessary to climb trees to achieve good, all-round observation. The Soviet soldier on the ground is armed with a PPSh submachine gun.

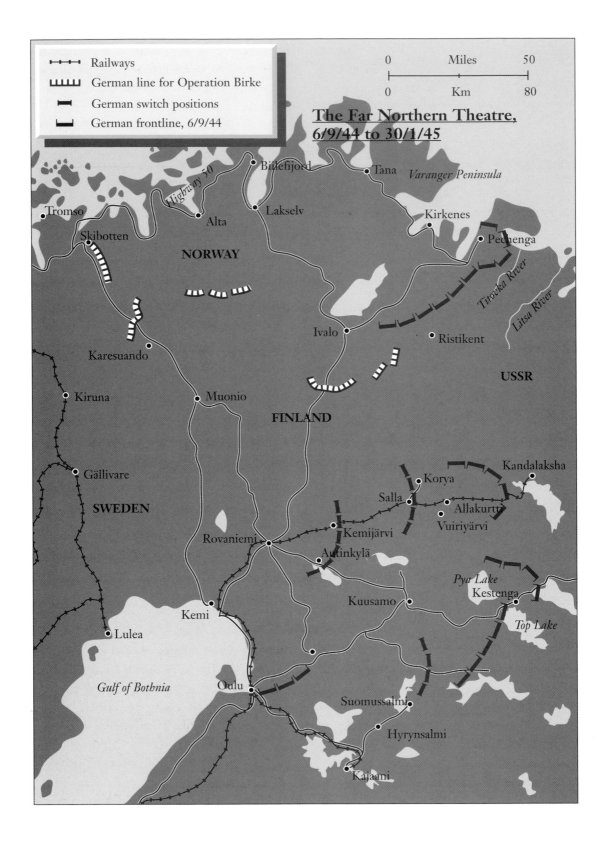

**The Far Northern Theatre,
6/9/44 to 30/1/45**

Railways
German line for Operation Birke
German switch positions
German frontline, 6/9/44

0   Miles   50
0   Km   80

Varanger Peninsula

Tromso
Skibotten
Alta
Billefijord
Lakselv
Tana
Kirkenes
Pechenga
Highway 50
NORWAY
Titovka River
Litsa River

Karesuando
Ivalo
Ristikent
USSR

Kiruna
Muonio
FINLAND

Gällivare
SWEDEN
Rovaniemi
Kemijärvi
Salla
Korya
Kandalaksha
Allakurtti
Vuiriyärvi
Autinkylä

Kuusamo
Pya Lake
Kestenga
Kemi
Top Lake

Lulea
Gulf of Bothnia
Oulu
Suomussalmi
Hyrynsalmi
Kajaani

in the Finnish panhandle – at Kilpisjärvi. Finland was finally rid of its ally turned enemy. But the price had been heavy: half of Lapland's reindeer (a vital food source and economic staple) had been killed, most towns and settlements had been burnt to the ground, and all forms of communication and infrastructure were crippled. Both sides had lost a large number of troops. Finnish losses amounted to 2900 wounded and 1000 dead. German losses are not known.

To Rendulic the Finns were a far from trivial problem to cope with, since they blocked his plans to retreat and thus save the precious mountain troops in Lapland. But his main headache was the Soviet forces being prepared to attack his exposed Twentieth Mountain Army along the Litsa Front. Here was the main danger to his army, and a danger that was growing by the day.

In October 1944 XIX Mountain Corps (that held the Arctic Front) consisted of the 210th Infantry Division (five fortress battalions) guarding the coast from Tarnet (at Jakobs River) to Tana in the west. Divisional Group *van der Hoop* held the front from the Petsamofjord to the mouth of the Titovka River. Thus it covered the Srednii Isthmus, which was the land bridge to the Fisher Peninsula proper. Not taking this strategic area back in 1941 was to cost the Germans dear, since the Russians had been using it to launch flank attacks against the German-held coast. It also lengthened Rendulic's front unnecessarily and made his troops' defensive task that more difficult. The actual Litsa Front was held from the coast down to Lake Chapr by the 6th Mountain Division and from Chapr to Hill 237.1 (the southernmost point of the front) by the 2nd Mountain Division (Lieutenant-General Hans Degen). All in all, XIX Mountain Corps (General Jodl) was, for the German Army of 1944, a formidable force with its divisions at 90 percent strength.

GERMAN DEFENCE LINES

The Germans relied upon fixed fortified lines of defence. The first was manned and the other two, behind the frontline, were to be used when and if the corps needed to fall back. All the hilltops in the line were fortified with concrete and steel reinforced bunkers, often with a system of depots, barbed wire and minefields to defend each one. Such strongpoints were held by platoons. The valleys in between were covered by minefields and trenches that could be manned in an emergency. The second defence line was west of the Titovka and the third one was on the Petsamo River. The Litsa Front's defences were reinforced a week before the Russians attacked, since the Germans knew with great accuracy when and where the Russians would attack.[16] But Hitler's usual stand-fast order for the troops was still the official order for the corps. Would these men, like their comrades at Stalingrad and El Alamein, be sacrificed by their Führer's intransigence?

It looked like they would until Hitler relented, probably because he wanted to save these élite troops for the defence of the ever-more-threatened Reich. On 3 October Hitler approved Operation *Nordlicht* (Northern Light): the retreat from

The Germans were able to make a general withdrawal through Rovaniemi and Salla and thence north without losing their organization or fighting capability.

Lapland by the Twentieth Mountain Army to the Lyngen position. It was an unprecedented decision. Never before had such a huge military force been evacuated during an Arctic winter. It meant coordinating three mountain corps from three widely dispersed directions: south, southeast and east. XIX Mountain Corps would have to use Highway 50, which was deemed impassable, due to snow, from 1 October to 1 June. The Mountain Army faced a potential Finno-Soviet pincer if their attacks were coordinated. Luckily for the Germans they were not. But Hitler had further worries. The precarious coastal road was an open invitation for the Western Allies to land a force on the Norwegian coast to cut off the German retreat. Such a landing might also trigger the ever-hostile Swedes to abandon neutrality and at the eleventh hour join the Allied side in the war.[17] Neither of these remote possibilities ever materialized, though.

The main reason the Germans got away was that the Allies and the USSR were too pre-occupied elsewhere to pursue this elusive quarry with the necessary vigour. Stalin, as with Finland, had larger and fatter territorial fish to fry, namely Poland, Hungary and Germany. In the Arctic he was satisfied with merely clearing the Germans from Soviet soil.

Stalin placed his confidence in Meretskov despite his "lacklustre" performance against Finland, and the marshal in his turn placed his confidence in his subordinate commanders. Lieutenant-General V.I. Shcherbakov, commander of the Fourteenth Army since 1942, had fought in the Winter War and was entirely trusted by Meretskov. The Fourteenth Army was made up of the following units: CXXVI Light Rifle Corps[18] (Colonel Solorev) – two brigades; CXXVII Light Rifle Corps (Major-General G.A. Zhukov) – two naval rifle brigades with plenty of combat experience

This long file of men is part of a battery of Red Army 82mm mortars. The simple construction and portability of these weapons made them an ideal substitute for artillery on the Arctic Front. The rearmost soldier carries the base plate.

Well-protected by the solid earth and timber of his trench, this Soviet officer is the very image of a combat soldier. Dressed in a crumpled gym-nastiovka, he is carefully observing no-man's land

from the Karelian offensive against the Finns but lacking in transport; XCIX Rifle Corps (Lieutenant-General Mikulsky) – three rifle divisions: 65th, 114th and 338th, all with combat experience from the Karelian Front; and CXXXI Rifle Corps (Major-General Alekseev) – 10th Guards Division and 14th Rifle Division.[19] These two divisions had been stationed in the Murmansk sector all along and were the only true Arctic veterans in the Fourteenth Army. Finally there was Major-General Absaliamov's XXXI Rifle Corps (83rd and 367th Rifle Divisions), transferred from Karelia but lacking in combat experience.

Like his colleagues, Meretskov placed great confidence in the tank. For the first time large amounts of armour were to be used in the Arctic. He had the following units at his disposal: 7th Guards Tank Brigade (37 T-34s), 89th Independent Tank Regiment (18 T-34s), 73rd Independent Guards Heavy Tank Regiment (21 KV-1s) and the 339th and 378th Guards Heavy Self-Propelled Artillery Regiments (34 JSU-152s). Compared to the tankless Germans this was a lavish amount of armour. But once again the Russians failed to take the terrain into account, and soon this armour proved itself to be of little use in the hilly, impassable, wet tundra landscape, confining the tanks to the roads where they made juicy and inviting targets for the German anti-tank guns and Stukas. They were more of a hindrance than a help on the Arctic Front, where it was horses and men who fought the war.

Of far greater importance than the armour was the Red Air Force. As the roads would not permit the swift and correct deployment of artillery to frontline units, great reliance was placed on the air force to provide "flying artillery support" for the advancing troops. While fighters (such as the La-5, Yak-3 and 9) were to cover the forward areas – by attacking withdrawing German units and enemy artillery positions – the bombers were to attack the Luftwaffe's airfields at Kirkenes, Salmijärvi and Luostari. The Luftwaffe's Fifth Air Fleet had 160 aircraft in total, half of which

were fighters, with a good many Stukas. But they faced Lieutenant-General Sokolov's formidable Seventh Air Army of 629 aircraft: 132 bombers, 189 dive-bombers and 308 fighters. Or in other words the Russians had a five to one superiority. Formidable odds indeed.[20]

Meretskov's army was far larger and his operations calculated to be far more ambitious than any previous ones, including the German offensive of 1941, and would place enormous demands upon the often ad-hoc and primitive Soviet supply system. But on this remote and climactically demanding front – the most remote of the Soviet fronts – not even the Russians could afford to be cavalier about supplies and food for their troops. Meretskov was provided with 30 engineering battalions (under Lieutenant-General Khrenov) with every form of equipment possible, including captured German pontoon bridges, British Bailey bridges and 300 assault boats. There were many rivers and lakes to be crossed, and the Germans could be trusted to have destroyed everything behind them.

Far more important at this distance and in these harsh surroundings were supplies. By early October the Fourteenth Army had accumulated 17,272 tonnes (17,000 tons) of ammunition, 3048 tonnes (3000 tons) of fuel and lubricants, and 50,000 dry rations to be air dropped to the troops during the advance. The troops were issued with two-day rations, the army depots had another week's supplies, and in Murmansk were stored another 10 days' supplies. The troops were also issued with sheepskin

A determined-looking Soviet soldier poses resolutely for the camera. It is interesting to note how well the man's camouflage suit blends in with the surroundings.

coats, extra-thick winter boots and thousands of white camouflage smocks. For heating, over 65,000 cubic metres (84,500 sq yd) of firewood had been stored in depots and camps. All these supplies were vitally needed if the momentum of the offensive was to be maintained. But their accumulation and stockpiling was one thing; getting them to where the troops actually were was an entirely different proposition and quite a headache for the high command. The Fourteenth Army needed 812 tonnes (800 tons) of supplies daily to function properly, and this was the minimum level in an army renowned for surviving on scant rations and irregular deliveries. (On other sectors of the Russian Front the troops were expected to live off the land. That was not possible in the Arctic.) A truck repair depot was set up and a special Road Service Corps, with seven truck battalions, was established. But this only took care of the road transport needs of the Fourteenth Army. For unit-to-unit delivery in the roadless wastes of the front the Russians (like the Finns and Germans) had to rely on dog sleighs, horses (carrying 112.5 kg/250lb each) and a horde of 500 reindeer (each carrying 33.8 kg/75lb). Although the reindeer had a lower carrying capacity it was more adapted to the deep snow, harsh cold and environment than the horse.

By early October 1944 all the preparations under way since the summer had been completed, enabling Meretskov to carry out Stalin's command: clear out the Germans, retake lost territory, capture the Petsamo Corridor (ceded by the Finns) and liberate eastern Finnmarken, including Kirkenes. The limits of this last objective would be decided upon by Stalin, who was reluctant to march into Norway both for political and strategic reasons and because the troops of the Fourteenth Army would soon be needed on the main front. Meretskov acted accordingly. He had over 100,000 troops, 2000 artillery pieces and heavy howitzers and almost 800 aircraft to destroy the enemy. And it was the German 2nd Division which would feel the full brunt of his army's weight.

AN UNSTOPPABLE RED TIDE

To the Russians artillery was the "God of War" and their offensives, like a Russian symphony, always opened with a heavy fanfare of artillery to soften up and demoralize the enemy before the infantry was sent in. At 08:00 hours on 7 October the artillery opened up, firing 10,000 rounds against the Litsa Front in two and a half hours. But low clouds, falling snows and fog prevented an accurate bombardment destroying the German defences. (Again and again the extremities of climate and natural surroundings would place obstacles in the way of the Russian offensive.) By the end of the day CXXXI Rifle Corps had established a bridgehead west of the Litsa, while XCIX Rifle Corps was still east of it. By the 8th it had reached the east bank of the river despite fierce German air attacks, while farther north CXXXI Corps had reached the Titovka River. The Germans had demolished the bridge but the engineers built a light pontoon bridge across at a furious pace, which enabled CXXXI Rifle Corps to expand its bridgehead. Farther south CXXVI LRC pushed across the Titovka without resistance: the atrocious terrain and deep snow which bogged down both men and horses was enough. Rendulic was aware of this "probe" but had no spare troops to block CXXVI Corps. The same route was taken by CXXVII LRC. Having started from a point farther east, its advance was a lot slower and was not completed until 9 October.

Rendulic ordered Jodl to begin withdrawing the 2nd Division to Luostari before it was surrounded and crushed by the advancing Russians, while the 6th Division was pulled back to Titovka. Here, Rendulic wanted Jodl to hold his position until he was able to get all his troops and supplies back to Norway.

But Meretskov was not giving up the chase and in fact speeded up his army's advance. At dawn on 9 October, XCIX Rifle Corps began to cross the Titovka on logs and at points which could be forded – an unenviable task given the freezing water and often heavy German fire. Russian dive-bombers could operate as the skies were clear and the weather fine – they cut German telephone lines (strung out along the roads) and interrupted the German retreat. But the lack of good roads was slowing the Soviet advance, proving that tanks could not be used in offroad terrain, while the lack of frontline artillery had to be compensated for by close air support. But that air cover depended upon the weather. One compensation was that the Russians could use their naval superiority to outflank the Germans by landings on the coast. During midnight on 9/10 October, the 63rd Naval Infantry Brigade landed on the opposite side of the Srednii Isthmus, while at 05:00 hours the following morning the 12th Naval Infantry Brigade crossed the German lines.

Jodl was not only forced to cancel a planned counterattack, but his entire corps now faced encirclement.

The fighting was now concentrated around

Behind Soviet lines the constant flow of food and ammunition continued to move despite the weather. Horse- or reindeer-drawn sledges were often more practical than wheeled vehicles on the tundra.

The mainstay of the Soviet tank armies during the middle years of the war, a T-34/76, probes cautiously forward. The sloped armour was particularly effective in reducing the damage done by German anti-tank guns.

Luostari, where the Russians where converging. During a gruelling five-day march CXXVII LRC arrived there with both exhausted horses and men. The Germans took advantage of this, and the 6th Division mounted an effective counterattack which delayed the Soviet capture of Kolosjoki (Nikel) long enough for the German engineers to carry out Rendulic's order to destroy the mines and process plant there. Rendulic also ordered the 163rd Division to move north to reinforce XIX Mountain Corps. Due to congested roads and stiff German resistance, it was not until noon on 12 October that Luostari – a crucial road junction – was finally captured. Elsewhere the Russians were making much slower progress, which allowed the Germans to retreat in relative peace. They were also helped by the arrival, after a chilling 400km (248-mile) journey northwards, of the 163rd (Engelbrecht) Division, which immediately upon arrival attacked the Russian position at Luostari on 12–13 October. Along the coast a vigorous German defence had slowed the Soviet advance, but the deadlock was broken during the evening of 12 October when 600 Russian marines landed inside the port of Liinahamari.

Reluctantly, Rendulic had agreed by the afternoon of 13 October that Jodl could retreat across the Norwegian border, but to do so he would have to capture the Norwegian hamlet of Tarnet on the frontier, which was held by the Soviet 72nd Naval Rifle Brigade. The Germans attacked and this allowed 18,000 of their troops (from the 2nd and 6th Divisions and Divisional Group *Hoop*) to escape westwards. After some heavy street fighting in Petsamo the Russians captured the town on 15 October. As the German stragglers escaped across the tundra, Shcherbakov ordered a halt to the offensive so that his troops could rest and regroup. In a mere nine days the Fourteenth Army had captured three key Arctic towns, crossed three major rivers and killed some 6000 Germans.

This halt gave Rendulic a chance to confer with General Reubel (commander of the 163rd Division) and Jodl. Rendulic expected (quite rightly) that it was Reubel's unit that would have to bear the brunt of the Soviet offensive when

it restarted, and he admonished his commanders to hold Kirkenes at all cost. Having been given Stavka permission to cross the Norwegian border, the 45th Rifle Division was the first across – that same afternoon – and it continued its advance down the road from Tarnet. Its progress was hampered by German strongholds on the hilltops and the lack of cover on the tundra. Again, the tanks accompanying the unit showed themselves to be completely unsuited to the terrain: trying to execute an enveloping movement they got bogged down in one of the numerous swamps that dotted the tundra.

The Germans were, however, not having it all their own way. Soviet marines (of the 12th Brigade again) landed on the coast and cut the road along which the 6th Mountain Division was retreating. Only by abandoning its vehicles could the Germans make their way across the tundra. On 22 October, XCIX Rifle Corps had reached the Pasvik and crossed this final river obstacle by using amphibious jeeps and rafts. By the following day

A Russian ski-patrol moves through a wintry scene. The first man carries a PPSh model 1941 7.62mm submachine gun, which was capable of firing at a rate of 900 rounds per minute.

the engineers had erected a pontoon bridge at Holmfoss and a second bridgehead had been established at Trangsund; both moves threatening the Kirkenes perimeter.

But it was farther south on the road between Luostari and Kolosjoki, that the heaviest fighting was taking place. The Russians found themselves up against the newly formed Battle Group *Reubel* (of the 163rd Division and Mountain Jägers – 15,000 troops in total). The Germans held Hill 441.4 against several poorly coordinated Russian attacks that suffered from lack of artillery, ammunition shortages and the ineffectiveness of their armoured support. All these problems were due to the lack of good roads.[21] It was only by 20 October that CXXVII Corps had managed to capture the airfield at Kolosjoki (Nikel) and inform a much-relieved Shcherbakov that the town was surrounded. The German garrison (of 1000) was caught unawares, and it was only by mounting a single, concentrated attack along the road – that left 850 Russians dead along it – that they managed to elude their pursuers. Two days later all German resistance in the Nikel region had ended, leaving the Fourteenth Army only 20km (12.4 miles) from the outskirts of Kirkenes. It was only a partial triumph for the Russians; although they had captured the mines the Germans had blown them up.

While the 163rd Division retreated southwards, the 6th Mountain Division had taken possession of Kirkenes; but how long could it hold out against the Fourteenth

Operated by a two-man crew, one clearly an Asiatic, the Soviet 50mm Model 1941 mortar had a maximum range of 600m (800yd) and could fire at a rate of 30 rounds per minute in battle.

Army's onslaught? CXXVI LRC captured Munkelv, which cut Highway 50 – the German escape route westwards from Kirkenes. At the same time Shcherbakov ordered XCIX Rifle Corps (from the south) and CXXXI Rifle Corps (from the east) to take Kirkenes in a classic pincer move. If CXXVI LRC held its position then the Germans would be trapped and crushed at Kirkenes. On 23 October, while the 45th Rifle Division crossed the Jarfjord in amphibious trucks, jeeps and in captured Norwegian fishing boats, CXXXI Rifle Corps advanced a mere 2km (1.24 miles) due to fierce German resistance. XCIX Rifle Corps made a swift crossing at Holmfoss and support-ed by armour (KVs and self-propelled guns) had reached 10km (6 miles) south of Kirkenes by the evening of 24 October. That same evening the Russians saw a fountain of flames and explosions coming from Kirkenes as the German sappers laid it waste. They did a thorough job of demolishing rails, the port facilities and burning down the houses in the city. The population (of 10,000) were not evacuated, as in other parts of Finnmarken, because the Germans did not have sufficient time to organize a seaborne evacuation. By the morning of 25 October three Soviet divisions had entered Kirkenes, fighting a fierce battle street by street with the German rearguard. By noon the Soviet

Mopping up in northern Norway in late 1944: a troop of T-60 light tanks fords a stream during a Soviet attack. Each vehicle is carrying several infantrymen, known as "tank desant" men. The infantry rode into battle on the backs of the tanks, jumping off to fight.

flag flew over the smouldering ruins of Kirkenes – the first city in Norway to be liberated from the Nazi occupiers. Two days later the Russian captured the ruined town of Neiden – where the Germans had only left the local church standing.

The last Arctic battles took place along the Pasvik River. On 23 October XXXI Rifle Corps was ordered south along the Arctic Highway, while Absaliamov's CXXVII LRC advanced south on the Norwegian side of the Pasvik. The advance was hampered by precarious supply lines, a lack of bridging material and the blown bridges the Germans had left behind. XXXI Rifle Corps managed to cross the Shuonjoki River across a pontoon bridge by the 25th, but the Russians were not able to dislodge the enemy from Mount Kaskama. By the time the final Russian attack came on 26 October the Germans had already managed to escape across the river, where CXXVII LRC had not kept pace with the advance due to a severe shortage of food. The only consolation was the capture of a large German supply depot at Maitolo (which was a welcome relief for the supply starved Russians) and the HP station at Nautsi on 29 October. That same day Meretskov called a halt to the Russian advance, and on 5 November the Russians made contact with the Finns at Ivalo. A week later forward elements of the 114th Rifle Division reached Tana, but advanced no further.

The Soviet offensive had come to an end, and although much valuable territory had been captured containing both ports and mines, Rendulic's army had escaped.[22]

A MASTERFUL WITHDRAWAL

Indeed, the Germans could be satisfied with *Nordlicht*: it had succeeded beyond their greatest expectations. German losses compared to other sections of the Eastern Front were relatively small: 22,000 troops out of Twentieth Mountain Army's total of 200,000. But the fighting retreat of this "undefeated army", as the Germans were to call it, had in fact cost them as many lives as Operation Silverfox back in 1941. On 2 November 2nd Mountain Division passed safely through Lakselv, the day after the Germans evacuated Ivalo, while the 139th Brigade still held Kautokeino. The Germans had completed *Nordlicht* by January 1945, but still held Alta and Hammerfest, which they occupied for another month.[23] It was the Norwegians and Finns who paid the price for this "splendidly executed and almost bloodless" German retreat across their northernmost province. Only the Laps (8500 nomads) and the population of Kirkenes escaped the forced German deportation. The rest – some 43,000 people – were evacuated by sea, since Highway 50 was clogged with the debris of the retreating German Army. Rendulic, remembered as the "Burner of Finnmarken", gave orders that no houses of any description were to be left behind: bridges, quays, ports, jetties and every ship that could not be taken was destroyed. Pleased with his troops' thoroughness, Rendulic proudly boasted that only 200 Norwegians had escaped the evacuation. But by the time he left for the Fatherland, in January 1945, the Nazi empire was crumbling fast. Soon the nightmare of war would come to an end, but not before the Russians had conquered Berlin with fire and sword.

Chapter 7

THE PRICE

OF

OCCUPATION

The German occupation of Norway had initially been beneficial to the Nazis, but in the end it was a failure in terms of resources extracted and the assimilation of Norwegian society into a greater German Reich.

The Germans had invaded Norway for sound enough strategic reasons. The necessity of denying possession of the country to Great Britain was clear enough and its capture provided the German Navy and Air Force with excellent bases from which to attack British maritime communications. Occupation also ensured that British control of the North Sea and the imposition of an economic blockade on Germany was made less effective. There were other reasons, too. Ensuring the continued supply of Swedish iron ore, which when the Baltic froze in winter had to come out of Narvik and be carried by sea down the Norwegian west coast, ranked high in Hitler's motivations.

A burning fish oil plant at Vagsoy during a British Commando raid in December 1941. These raids convinced Hitler that the British were planning an invasion of Norway.

Norway also contained other useful minerals and economic resources that could be exploited. The large Norwegian fishing fleet might provide a useful source of food for Germany's armies and population. On the ideological front Alfred Rosenberg, the Nazi theorist, hoped that as a suitably "pure" Aryan race, the Norwegians could usefully and willingly be incorporated in to the "Greater German Reich".

In the aftermath of *Weserübung*, therefore, the Germans could have few doubts about the wisdom of invading Norway. The Kriegsmarine had suffered heavily, which had long-term implications, but, all in all, the campaign had been stunning success, achieved at limited cost and at no detriment to Plan *Gelb* – the attack on France. The British, French and Norwegians had been thoroughly defeated, providing a useful psychological boost and further convincing Hitler of his own military genius.[1] However, its issue did not prove quite so simple. On the whole the Norwegian population were sullenly uncooperative and at times the Norwegian resistance movement caused the Germans considerable difficulties. Granted that the possession of Norway gave Germany many economic benefits, Hitler's conviction that Norway was the "'zone of destiny' in this war" undermined these benefits.[2] He was convinced the British intended to invade and thus gave disproportionate emphasis to Norway's defence. The resources tied up in Norway, in men, ships, aircraft and materiel, could have been far better used elsewhere.

Aryan "brothers in arms": Norwegians in the Nordland *Regiment on the Leningrad Front in 1942.*

The German military required a stable base in Norway, and the commander of German forces in Norway, General Nikolaus von Falkenhorst, had no wish to divert troops to undertake "anti-partisan" style operations. The efficient exploitation of Norway's mineral and fishing resources also required calm. The Germans were keen, therefore, to establish some kind of stable regime to avoid unnecessary upheaval. Quisling's coup attempt of 9 April 1940 and his call to his countrymen to lay down their arms had done little more than stiffen Norwegian resistance. As a result, the Germans had sidelined him and established an Administrative Council to deal with civil affairs in the areas under their control.

Heinrich Himmler, head of the SS, was enthusiastic about incorporating Norwegian volunteers in the Waffen-SS.

On 24 April 1940, Hitler sent Joseph Terboven to Norway to act as Reichkommissar, a position of considerable power. His tasks were two-fold: to further German war aims and to establish an effective occupation government. He hoped to achieve the latter by legal means, ideally by having the *Storting*, the Norwegian parliament, depose the king, set up a government that would cooperate with him and then meekly dissolve itself. The Norwegian parliamentarians, given the situation in Europe at the time in the summer of 1940, proved acquiescent. That June, in their least finest hour, they appealed to King Haakon to abdicate in favour of a new council in the occupied country. Haakon steadfastly refused, but this did not stop them voting 75 to 55 to remove their king on

10 September 1940. However, talks between Terboven and the *Storting* went less well, and Terboven was forced to establish a German commissarial government and return Quisling, championed by Raeder and Rosenberg, to a prominent role. Terboven had failed to use the Norwegian legal system to produce a constitutional collaborationist government.[3]

The failure legally to sideline King Haakon also had serious long-term implications. On 18 July 1940 he rejected the June parliamentary request for his abdication. He emphasized the legitimacy of his government, now in exile in London, and stated it had received its mandate to continue the struggle at the last free parliament held on 9 April.[4] The king's stance and subsequent conduct made him a focus of unity and inspiration for the vast majority of the Norwegian population. This was a significant challenge to German control and had military implications, too. The Norwegian resistance never questioned its loyalty to the king or government and, its military wing, Milorg, (*Militæroganasjonen* – The Military Organization), came under the direct control of the Norwegian government-in-exile in February 1942, which did much to establish its legitimacy with the Norwegian population.[5]

Red Army soldiers in northern Norway in mid-1945. The soldier on the far right is wearing traditional Russian Army shoulder straps, pogoni, which were re-introduced by Stalin in 1943.

To the occupiers Quisling turned into something of liability. Terboven reckoned Quisling's party, the *Nasjonal Samling* (NS), was inefficient and absurdly small. However, the NS was all he had to work with and therefore the NS dominated the Commissarial State Council, although the real power lay with the German-staffed Reichskommissariat. Quisling initially chose not to join the council, but he remained the driving force behind the NS. Yet on 1 February 1942 he became minister-president, as the NS – in theory at least – was handed control in Norway by Terboven. Although thwarted in his desire for a peace treaty and subsequent alliance with Germany, Quisling put much effort into expanding the NS and attempting the Nazification of Norwegian society. On the former the projected 100,000 members failed to materialize, although the 35,000 achieved by late 1941 was reasonably respectable in the context of Norwegian politics. The latter proved more difficult. Quisling might well claim to Terboven that: "In hardly any other country is it as easy to bring about national revolution from above as it is in Norway." This was because the Norwegians were a law-abiding and stable people who if "given a well-reasoned argument for change . . . will soon accept it."[6] Yet practical experience proved his belief unfounded.

Vidkun Quisling (centre), leader of the Norwegian fascists. His efforts to Nazify Norway were a dismal failure.

So Quisling's efforts to establish the "New Order" in Norway met with little success. His attempt to place all Norwegian sport under NS control led to a wholesale

boycott of organized competition for the duration of the war, a sacrifice of considerable proportions for a nation so devoted to sport. The Norwegian church proved no easier to intimidate. Quisling's attempt to introduce a new catechism mentioning the necessity of "obedience to leader and state" led to the resignation of Norway's bishops and almost 90 percent of the Norwegian clergy. The NS could not fill the vacated posts. The bishops wrote to Terboven, appealing over the head of Quisling. The Reichskommissar cheerfully took the opportunity to embarrass the Norwegian, and replied with remarkable moderation – earlier he had rounded up 300 trade union members and executed their leaders – that he "desired a relaxation of tension" and advised Quisling that "clemency should be exercised."[7] The new catechism was dropped, the clergy returned to work, and the churches filled again. Terboven expressly forbad Quisling to press the deep-sea fishermen's and farmers' association to accept NS control because their work was so vital. Even after he was made minister-president, Quisling's standing did not increase. He made a determined effort to inculcate National Socialist values on Norwegian society through the elementary and secondary schools curricula, but this unleashed such a storm of protest that Terboven reined him in once more. The Reichkommissar's efforts to provide a stable and legitimate collaborationist government, which would ensure stability on the home front, had been an obvious failure.

The establishment of the Quisling regime's legitimacy might have provided the Germans with a useful source of manpower. After all, to quote Norwegian historian Olav Riste, the Norwegians had the "dubious honour of being regarded as a kindred folk, a wayward Nordic tribe that should be led into the greater German Reich through persuasion."[8]

Hitler was obsessed with an Allied invasion of Norway, and so reinforced the garrison to ludicrous levels.

Quisling discussed the idea of Norwegian military support for Germany, specifically in the SS, in Berlin in December 1940. The Standarte *Nordland* had been formed by the head of the SS, Heinrich Himmler, in May 1940 but it was officially announced to Norway in January 1941 by Quisling who proclaimed that, "Germany has not asked us to come. We ourselves feel duty-bound to march freely and firmly to the very end along the road which destiny has marked for our people. Norway and Germany have common interests. Germany's victory is Norway's victory."[9] After the invasion of the Soviet Union, the Norwegian SS volunteers, now in the Norwegian Legion, saw service around Leningrad. The legion's 2000 men took massive casualties in the fighting of 1942, and it was disbanded in May 1943.

NORWEGIAN SS VOLUNTEERS

The majority of the surviving legionnaires immediately re-enlisted in the Panzergrenadier Regiment *Norge*. Officially this was intended to be a solely Norwegian-manned unit, but it had to be topped up with Hungarian and Romanian volunteers. It was part of the 11th SS Panzergrenadier Division *Nordland* and saw service in Yugoslavia, and was then despatched back to the Leningrad Front in December 1943. It took terrible losses holding the River Narva against the Soviet advance in the summer of 1944, and was encircled in the Courland Pocket in January 1945. The survivors numbering a few hundred were evacuated by sea, only to be annihilated in the battle for Berlin in April–May 1945. The SS Ski Battalion *Norge* was also formed and served with the 6th SS Mountain Division in Lapland. It returned to Norway when the Twentieth Mountain Army was forced out of Finland in September 1944. Some 5000 Norwegians served with the SS on the Eastern Front. As a purely military contribution, in that vast attritional struggle, these Norwegian forces were of minimal importance. They tended to "disappear into the maelstrom". The troops were high quality; their devotion and high number of casualties prove this, but Norway hardly provided a vast pool of suitably Aryan military manpower for the Greater German Reich's struggle against Bolshevism.[10]

Quisling, however, attached considerable political importance to Norway's military contribution. He also intended to build an army of his own, in an effort to prove his worth as a useful and loyal ally of Germany. He suggested that rather than relying on volunteers he would be able to conscript 60,000 men for service on the Eastern Front. Although the issue languished for some time, by January 1944 Quisling and his minister of justice, Sverre Riisnaes, had increased the number to 75,000. Riisnaes, at least, had few illusions about the enthusiasm for such an idea, reckoning that the borders would have to be sealed and defaulters rounded up by the German Army. The Norwegian Labour Service was the most likely institution to provide the machinery for the process. When the resistance discovered the plan, it issued a call to boycott registration for the service. By May 1944 thousands of young men had fled to the forests, mountains and Sweden. The regime's final attempt to

enforce "labour mobilization" was to withhold ration cards from those that did not register.[11] Then the resistance seized a lorry load of ration cards (some 150,000) and after this the labour mobilization scheme was quietly dropped.[12] Clearly Quisling failed in his effort to make Norway a useful ally of Nazi Germany. There was no eager participation in the Greater Reich as the Nazi theorist Rosenberg had hoped, nor was there any major manpower contribution to the German war effort – previously, Norwegian recruitment to the Waffen-SS was comparatively small by the standards of occupied Europe.

One of the key motivations for the German invasion was the economic benefit of occupying Norway. Long-term German plans were aimed at the exploitation of the country's mineral resources and hydro-electric power, but as the pressure of the war began to tell, particularly after 1942, the Germans became more concerned with meeting immediate goals, particularly with regard to maintaining their massive military presence in the country. There was a plethora of minerals to be found in Norway and a reasonably large aluminium industry. Soon much of this wealth was flowing to Germany, but never in the quantities anticipated. The Germans planned to increase Norwegian aluminium production to more than 243,840 tonnes (240,000 tons) a year. However, only 18,288 tonnes (18,000 tons) reached Germany in 1940, and this amount was never subsequently equalled. Of course the possession of the Norwegian coast also facilitated the traffic of Swedish iron ore, which was of absolutely crucial

Hot pursuit! A horse-drawn Soviet Model 1927 regimental gun moves up to support the infantry who are already engaged in fighting for the smoke-shrouded town in the distance in northern Norway in mid-1945.

importance to the German war economy and this eventually became the major deployment of Germany's merchant shipping. Furthermore, the Norwegian fishing industry provided Germany with much fish oil and glycerine. However, Allied action against the Norwegian fishing fleet and industry prevented it from making up more than half the German shortfall. As to Norwegian agricultural production, this had to be supplemented by imports, but the country was obliged to send a considerable part of its high-protein foodstuffs to Germany. The Norwegian standard of living dropped further than that of any of the other Scandinavian countries.[13]

SOE OPERATIONS IN NORWAY

Milorg was largely passive in the first years of occupation but Britain's Special Operations Executive (SOE), which had been set up to aid and support European resistance, undertook a number of operations against the strategically important industries. Norwegian Commandos of Company Linge attacked the iron pyrite mines at Orkla near Trondheim in February and October 1943, and the Stord mines near Bergen in November 1943. They also assaulted the Arendal silicon carbide foundry in November 1943. The most famous action was taken against the Norsk Hydro Heavy Water plant at Vemork, near Rjukan, in Telemark province. Heavy water is an effective moderator for slowing down neutrons in an atomic pile, and when the British discovered that the Germans had increased production and by implication were working on an atomic bomb, they were seriously worried. A Norwegian commando team led by Joachim Rønneberg attacked and destroyed the plant in February 1943. A USAAF air raid and further SOE action ensured that production was halted and remaining stocks could not be transferred to Germany. Although there is some debate as to the significance of the operation, it is worth quoting SOE's official historian M.R.D. Foot: "If SOE had never done anything else, 'Gunnerside' [the heavy water operation] would have given it claim enough on the gratitude of humanity."[14]

Hitler was convinced of the importance of maintaining control on Norway. He told Raeder, the C-in-C of the German Navy, that "if the British go about things properly they will attack northern Norway at several points . . . take Narvik if possible, and thus exert pressure on Sweden and Finland. This might be decisive for the war."[15] The British seriously investigated the possibility of retaking Norway on a number of occasions and, despite Winston Churchill's enthusiasm for such a project, rejected the possibility. As General Sir Alan

The never-ending routine of patrolling on the Arctic Front. The rather bulbous head shape is caused by the Red Army soldiers' practice of wearing their fur caps under their white snow suits.

Brooke, the British Chief of the Imperial General Staff, noted: "Heaven knows what we should have done in Norway had we landed there!"[16] Anyway, the American commanders were determined that the Anglo-American invasion would be launched against France. As General Fredrick Morgan, who headed the early planning for Operation Overlord said: "We went to Normandy or we stayed at home."[17]

This did not mean that the British were unwilling to operate in Norway. The Combined Operations organization launched a series of raids against the Norwegian coast in 1941.

BRITISH COMMANDO RAIDS

In March 1941, British Commandos landed on the Lofoten Islands and over the course of the operation destroyed large quantities of herring oil intended for Germany, and captured German troops and Norwegian collaborators. Meanwhile Royal Navy ships attacked shipping. In December, simultaneous assaults were launched against Vagsoy on the west coast, where the British were met by serious resistance, and again against Lofoten. These raids of 1941 caused economic damage of minimal importance and were launched essentially to gain experience in amphibious operations and for propaganda purposes.[18] Hitler, however, was inclined to imbue these operations with a significance that they did not deserve. At the Führer conference of 22 January, in the aftermath of the December raids, he declared that the country was "of decisive importance for the outcome of the war and ordered most of the German surface fleet to Norway."[19] The number of German troops in Norway increased dramatically from 100,000 at the beginning of 1942 to 250,000 by the summer. Hitler also ordered the construction of the Atlantic Wall, a line of defences "from the Pyrenees to the North Cape", and after the British raids he gave personal priority to the building and equipping of Norway's defences. This gave impetus to the construction of over 350 coastal forts and 20 or so airfields and, subsequently, radar stations. For example, a 96km (60-mile) stretch of coast in central Norway containing no major strategic towns contained 55 artillery pieces of calibres of 75mm to 155mm.[20] Given Erwin Rommel's concerns about the poor state of the Atlantic Wall in France, these resources would have been better used in more vital areas. The raiding continued in 1942, but on a far smaller scale given the increase in German defences.

Great Britain also viewed Norway as a useful target for deception operations. As Sir John Masterman, who was heavily involved in British deception planning, recalled: "Norway was the favourite playground for deception and even the most retentive memory would have difficulty in recalling just when and how often [we] put into effect a threat against that country."[21] At least three major deception plans were launched against Norway between 1941 and 1943. On the whole it is difficult to determine their effect, although German military resources in

A British Commando watches Maaloy burn during a raid in December 1941.

Norway continued to increase. The most important deception operation was "Fortitude", undertaken in support of the Allied invasion of Normandy. The key to the operation was "Fortitude South", which convinced the Germans that the main Allied effort was to be directed against the Pas de Calais rather than Normandy. "Fortitude North" was aimed against Norway. It was a complex operation; General Sir Andrew Thorne was given command of the notional Fourth Army, which would simulate a threat to Stavanger and Narvik. Thorne's

Soviet officers inspect the remains of a German anti-tank gun position in Norway. The gun is a 75mm Pak 40, which was capable of destroying almost any Russian tank.

Part of the German Army in Norway: the shattered remains of a German gun and its tractor, a Hanomag SdKfz 7, at the end of the war.

appointment gave additional weight to the plan, as he was personally known to Hitler, having met the Führer on several occasions as military attaché in Berlin during 1932–35.[22] However, the bulk of the deception was created by a team of radio operators who simulated the Fourth Army's preparations and British-controlled double agents. The impression the Germans had of the Fourth Army and its "purpose" was essentially as the British intended. The 12 German divisions in Norway stayed where they were, but they were not reinforced. On 1 March 1944 Fremde Heere West (FHW – Army High Command Foreign Armies West) considered that:

"Seeing that what the enemy leadership is up to at the present stage of operations is to do everything to tie down German forces on subsidiary fronts; and indeed divert them from the decisive Atlantic Front; and seeing that they have already tried to do this in Italy, it seems possible that they have decided to do this in the Scandinavian region."[23]

This was an accurate assessment of Allied intentions, but the FHW believed that the Fourth Army was an actual formation and they expected a diversionary thrust, even though they knew the main effort must come across the English Channel. The size of the German presence in Norway was largely down to the threat of an Anglo-American invasion. Although the many alarms and reinforcements can be attributed to raiding and the Germans mistaking Arctic convoys for invasion fleets, the contribution of the deception efforts added to German worries. However, having said all this, given Hitler's obsession with Norway, the troops would have probably been there whatever the Allies did.

END GAME

In the autumn of 1944 Finland withdrew from the war and in the face of Finnish pressure on their erstwhile ally and the Soviet offensive on the Murmansk Front, the German Twentieth and Twenty-First Mountain Armies withdrew into northern Norway. By January 1945 there were 15 German divisions in Norway. Even though the collapse of the German position in Finland distorted the situation, this was an extraordinary number of formations given the pressure the Wehrmacht was under on both the Eastern and Western Fronts at the time. Naturally the Germans tried to move these troops onto the continent, but in this they were severely hampered by the activities of Milorg.

More than 1000 Milorg members, trained and equipped by SOE, cut the tracks of Norway's vulnerable railway system and destroyed 10 bridges. Further confusion was created by Gunner Sønsterby of the famous Oslo Gang, who blew up the five-storey building housing the German railway administration staff in Oslo, burying their records. Rail traffic was delayed on average by a month.[24]

A DRAIN ON RESOURCES

There were still almost 400,000 Germans in Norway as the war drew to an end – a major military force. There had been much Allied speculation in April 1945 about the Germans fighting on in a *Festung Norwegen*. General Dwight Eisenhower, the Anglo-American supreme commander, even brought up the issue with Anglo-American Combined Chiefs of Staff. Terboven, an ardent Nazi, was in favour of fighting on but by then it was the military in Norway that truly held power. Admiral Dönitz, who had succeeded Hitler as Führer on 1 May 1945 following Hitler's suicide, made General Böhme supreme commander in Norway that same day, giving him formal command of the fleet and air force in addition to the army. Although Böhme might claim that "we stand in Norway unbeaten, and in possession of our full power. No enemy has dared attack us", he was disinclined to disobey the German High Command's order to accept unconditional surrender. So he concluded in his message to his troops on 7 May 1945 that, "we must nonetheless bow to his dictate, in consideration of the common interest."[25] The British were well aware that: "We certainly have not enough [troops] to deal with any concerted resistance."[26] Böhme dismissed Terboven, one possible source of trouble, but Quisling, in theory at least, had 15,000 armed men at his disposal. The police were also armed and the Norwegian SS ski battalion remained in Norway. However, there was no appetite for a final showdown amongst Quisling's supporters. Most, like their leader, waited meekly for the arrival of the Allies. Terboven chose suicide. The British General Sir Andrew Thorne was able to peacefully liberate Norway from 400,000 German personnel with a force of 30,000 men supplemented by 40,000 Milorg men.

There were definite advantages for the German occupation of Norway. For example, important bases were gained and the supply of Swedish iron ore was ensured. The exploitation of Norwegian mineral and fishing resources did not meet expectations, but were certainly useful additions to the Nazi cause. However, Quisling's intention of fully mobilizing Norway to the German cause was a hopeless failure. All that can be said of his contribution to the German occupation was that he was something of a "lighting conductor" for the Germans. As Finn Støren, Quisling's foreign policy advisor, told him in March 1945: "I have a feeling that the German authorities are deliberately making fools of you . . . and of the *Nasjonal Samling* . . . Under a pretence of friendship

The beginning of the long march into Soviet captivity for this group of German soldiers. Repatriation of POWs in the USSR did not begin until the early 1950s.

of cooperation, they manage to make our administration share their guilt as plunderers and oppressors."[27]

On the whole the Norwegian resistance was fairly passive. Norway was no Yugoslavia. However, there is no doubt that Norway was far too heavily occupied; there was one German for every ten Norwegians. This was largely due to Hitler's belief of Norway's importance in the war. This was a waste of German resources which could have been much better used elsewhere.

Conclusion

HITLER'S WAR IN THE FAR NORTH

After early German success in Norway in 1940, the war in the far north of Europe was characterized by Hitler's lack of judgement at all levels, whether in terms of strategy or understanding Finnish intentions.

General Eduard Dietl said in 1941: "There has never been a war fought in the high north." There were very good reasons why this was the case, as the European Arctic was in his opinion a miserable "desert" of a place in both summer and winter, with appalling communications, making the area "unsuited to military operations."[1] Yet in World War II the demands of Total War brought modern conflict to Scandinavia and the Arctic. There were important strategic assets in the region and that was enough to turn the attention of Europe's dictators, Hitler and Stalin, northwards. Although their strategic motivation was sound enough, many of the decisions they took

Nazi dictator Adolf Hitler (left) with Finnish leader Marshal Mannerheim (right). The latter was a Finnish nationalist first, and had no interest in an ideological war with the USSR.

with regard to Scandinavia and the Arctic had disastrous implications. Hitler claimed that Norway was "the 'zone of destiny' in this war."[2] It was not, but his obsession with the region made it more important and consumed more vital German resources than was necessary. This dispersion of effort was important within the context of the war as whole.

The war in the far north also threw up a whole raft of problems at both the operational and tactical level. Much has been made in this study of the difficulties of combat in the terrain and environment of the Arctic. How far these problems were solved, how well the soldiers, sailors and airmen from Germany, Finland, the Soviet Union, Great Britain and others adapted to the conditions they faced, and how well they were led decided whether or not the strategic goals of Hitler were met. It was the Allies that met the difficulties better. This is not to denigrate the efforts of the German forces in the area. They were hampered by a lack of resources, leadership and very often numbers. In consequence the German experience of war in the Arctic was, with the exception of the Norwegian campaign, largely negative, and despite the importance that Hitler gave to the region, very little was achieved.

Scandinavia was dragged into World War II by Hitler's strategic needs. Initially, however, this was due to his aims elsewhere in Europe that also gave his fellow totalitarian dictator, Joseph Stalin, an opportunity to address a number of Soviet defence

The approach waters to the port of Hanko. Ceded to the Soviets after the Winter War, it was a valuable naval base for Russian operations in the Baltic Sea.

*An aged naval gun on the out-
skirts of Leningrad. Finnish
reluctance to press the siege of
the city to the north was
a crucial factor in its survival.*

issues. Hitler needed a free hand to attack Poland and, subsequently, did not want to
have to worry about his eastern frontiers when he turned his attention westwards to
deal with Great Britain and France. Stalin, troubled by Japanese ambitions on the
Mongolian-Manchurian border, also wanted to avoid a two-front war, and specifically a war with Hitler. An accommodation with Hitler would also enable Stalin to
bolster Soviet security by securing a buffer zone on the Soviet Union's western border as insurance against future aggression. Stalin and Hitler were therefore able
come to the mutually advantageous Nazi-Soviet Pact of 23 August 1939. War followed nine days later. Hitler was able to pursue his ambitions against Poland and the
West without fear of Soviet interference. Likewise, Stalin could seek to expand westwards: the Soviets took their part of Poland, consumed the Baltic States and sought
to ensure the security of Leningrad, the outskirts of which lay within artillery range
of the Finnish border, by absorbing Finland into the Soviet empire.

Hitler's ambitions elsewhere had brought war to the far north, as the strategic balance in the region had been tipped by the German-Soviet understanding. Stalin took
the opportunity provided and the Red Army attacked Finland on 31 November

1939. This short, bloody war – the Winter War – also had serious implications for the future. The Soviets had expected an easy victory but the remarkable resistance put up by the Finns led to a reassessment of their strategic goals. They reorganized their military, concentrating the weight of their attack in the key area of the Karelian Isthmus, and also accepted the more limited objectives such as the capture of the isthmus and establishment of a naval base at Hanko. This was the basis of the peace settlement signed between Finland and the Soviet Union on 13 March 1940. A lot of lessons were drawn from the Winter War and many of those lessons were wrong. The diabolical performance of the Red Army in the first weeks of the war was duly noted by the German military, and thus could be breezily added to the whole raft of

As Finnish president, Marshal Mannerheim secured terms from the Soviets which left Finland independent.

evidence that German staff studies used to prove that victory could be achieved in the Soviet Union in eight to ten weeks.[3] They failed to note the improved performance of Timoshenko's troops in combined-arms operations, which broke the Mannerheim Line in late February and early March 1940. Indeed, it arguable that the reforms and rethinking undertaken by the Soviet military in the light of the Winter War led to the vastly improved performance of the Red Army in 1943–45.[4] Nor did they take into account the sheer tenacity of the Soviet soldier and the extraordinary ability of Red Army troops to fight on in the most hopeless situations. The Finns took note, the Germans did not, and such desperate

Red Army troops during the Winter War. Berlin took notice of their dismal performance, but failed to take into account Red Army reforms afterwards.

resistance would delay and wear down the German advance once the invasion of the Soviet Union was launched in June 1941.

The war also shaped Finland's attitude to both the Soviet Union and Germany, and Finland would be crucial to Hitler's Arctic war. Understandably, the war embittered the Finns in the period after the Peace of Moscow. Finland found itself isolated and fearful of future Soviet ambitions. Consequently the Finnish Government was open to German suggestions that Finland join in a renewed war against the Soviet Union. However, Finland was never a particularly reliable ally. Indeed, Finland baulked at the term "ally" preferring the term "co-belligerent", and was careful to allow the Soviet Union to begin hostilities. Hence Finland claimed that the war was ostensibly defensive and a "continuation" of the Winter War. On the whole the Finnish Government and military had considerable distaste for Nazism, and Mannerheim ensured that, prior to the opening of Operation Barbarossa, Heinrichs should make clear to the Germans that there should be no interference in Finland's internal politics.[5] Finland would cooperate in Germany's attack on the USSR, but the country was determined to maintain its independence.

Time and time again the Finns demonstrated their determination not to be Germany's pawn in the war against the Soviet Union. There was little cooperation in the opening of the war in the Arctic, as the Finns did not want to provoke Stalin, and thus Dietl's advance on Murmansk did not begin until 29 June 1941, a week after the main invasion of the USSR, and he was denied the vital element of surprise. In November 1941, Siilavuo's III Corps shifted to the defensive despite its successes in Lapland, in direct contravention of German wishes. This was probably because Mannerheim did not want to alienate the Western powers by advancing too far into the USSR. The failure to cut the northern branch of the Murmansk railway, for similar reasons, was of vital strategic importance. Mannerheim refused to use Finnish troops to help the German advance on Kandalaksha. Nor did the Finns crush the Soviet base at Hanko, but rather were content to allow the Soviets to evacuate it on 2 December. Most importantly, Finnish forces did not push beyond the pre-Winter War border on the Karelian Isthmus, nor did they advance past the River Svir and complete the encirclement of Leningrad. Mannerheim refused to become involved in the siege, and this was absolutely crucial to the eventual failure of the Germans to take the USSR's second city. Finland was no more helpful in 1942, refusing Dietl's pleas for a renewal of the offensive, and once again in May Siilasvuo halted his counteroffensive early.

SHIFTS IN FINNISH POLICY

After Stalingrad in February 1943, Finland's leaders realized that a German defeat was inevitable and re-established contacts with the Soviets. The intermittent negotiations broke down in February 1944, but the massive Soviet offensive of June 1944 forced Finland out of the war. Mannerheim stabilized the front with the help of emergency aid purchased from Germany. In return Ryti, the Finnish president, gave an undertaking that Finland would not make a separate peace. However, after the Soviets shifted troops away from Finland for the drive on Germany, Mannerheim replaced Ryti and promptly reneged on the promise. To the disgust of Hitler, Finland made that separate peace and subsequently used force to evict German forces from its territory. Caught between two dictators, Finland managed the astonishing feat of avoiding occupation and emerged from World War II as an independent state.

The Winter War had drawn Hitler's attention to Anglo-French interest in Norway. He certainly could not allow the Western Allies to establish themselves there due to the threat to Germany's Baltic coast. Quite apart from this essentially reactive reason, there were sound strategic motives for capturing the country. It would ensure the vital supply of Swedish iron ore. Norway also contained plentiful resources, an extensive hydro-electric industry and large fishing fleet, all of which

Norwegian ships lie damaged in port following a German Stuka attack in April 1940. The German invasion of Norway was a brilliant combined-arms operation.

might make a useful contribution to the German war economy. Most important of all, Norway could provide useful air and naval bases, possession of which would hamper the British blockade of Germany and allow Germany to make attacks on British maritime supply routes and, in particular, provide easier access to the Atlantic.

And so Hitler launched Operation *Weserübung* on 9 April 1940. It was an astounding success. In the first true combined operation, the Kriegsmarine, Luftwaffe and German Army decisively beat the Norwegians and their ill-prepared British and French allies. British naval superiority was obviated by surprise and German air power. On the ground the Germans demonstrated considerable tactical flexibility and skill in difficult conditions to overcome their opponents. Within two months the Germans won a decisive victory and secured the Scandinavian minerals, the Narvik iron ore route and the naval bases that the head of the German Navy, Raeder, had wanted so much. Hitler reckoned he had won an important psychological victory over the British and French. It was not without cost, however, given the losses suffered by the Kriegsmarine. This hampered any full exploitation of the strategic situation and the capture of the French Atlantic ports lessened, at least initially, the importance of Norway as a German naval base.

The benefits of the occupation of Norway never fully lived up to German expectations. The Norwegian people steadfastly resisted attempts to Nazify their society, so there was no smooth integration of a "kindred people" into the Greater German Reich, so hoped for by Nazi theorist Alfred Rosenberg. Nor did the exploitation of Norway's natural resources fully meet German targets. These were minor issues, however, compared to Hitler's obsession with protecting his conquest from Anglo-American recapture. Between the middle of 1941 and June 1944 there were nine to twelve German divisions in Norway. While the quality of these formations was variable, there is no doubt Norway was utterly over-garrisoned. There was one German to every ten Norwegians, making for the highest level of occupation in Europe. While this ensured the Norwegian resistance movement was passive for most of the war, it is clear that at least some of the 400,000 German servicemen in Norway by the end of the war could have been better used elsewhere.

Most significant of all was the fact that Norway saw the largest deployment of the German surface fleet. Hitler's retreat from Atlantic raiding after the sinking of the *Bismarck* meant that – apart from its

Vidkun Quisling, whose name was to become synonymous with traitorous collaboration with the enemy.

German troops in mud on the Arctic Front. In general, the Germans had great difficulty adapting to the conditions found in Karelia.

role as a "fleet-in-being", ensuring the Royal Navy's Home Fleet was equipped with aircraft carriers and modern battleships which might be more better employed in other theatres – the most useful contribution that the German surface fleet could make was to attack the Arctic convoys. This was an utterly crucial strategic imperative. The Germans always saw the naval war in the Arctic as an adjunct to the war on the Eastern Front. This was because there was little doubt that the supplies brought in to Murmansk by the Allied merchant ships were vital to the Soviet war economy. The special alloys, trucks, jeeps, communications equipment, particularly radios and waterproof telephone wire, high-octane aviation fuel and a whole host of other vital goods ensured the Soviets weathered the German offensives of 1941–43, and could shift to the attack in 1944–45. Although Soviet industry proved good at producing tanks, it struggled to produce even a decent truck in large numbers and certainly not any of the more sophisticated items mentioned above.

This was of war-winning significance, which the Germans recognized and thus the passage of the convoys had to be halted. However, German efforts to do so floundered in the face of fuel shortages, timid leadership, poorly drawn conclusions from combat experience and the élan of the Royal Navy. It is almost inconceivable that the Germans did not cause the British inordinate problems. Yet the German surface ships often failed to press their advantage, such as in the Battle of the Barents Sea, or blundered into British traps, such as in the case of the *Scharnhorst*. The Luftwaffe drew the wrong conclusions from the destruction of convoy PQ17, and suffered accordingly when it attacked PQ18. Thus the Germans suffered serious losses amongst their experienced torpedo bomber crews and amongst their specialized anti-shipping aircraft. Their crews, despite suffering from poor morale due to the long periods of inaction, fought bravely when required but as prophesied by Raeder at the start of the war, they did indeed "die gallantly" in their thousands aboard the *Scharnhorst* and *Tirpitz*.

There were also good strategic reasons for attacking on land in the Arctic once Barbarossa opened. It would secure the supply of Finnish nickel from the mines around Nautsi. Most importantly, however, was the capture of Murmansk, which would cut the Soviets off from their vital supply route with the Western Allies. Yet, as the German High Command was convinced that the Soviets would be defeated within two to four months, too few troops were committed to the assault. Hitler further dispersed their efforts by setting them three goals rather than concentrating on a single achievable objective. In addition, the delay in launching Silverfox allowed the Soviets to build up their defences, and when the fighting broke out the Soviet troops put up a remarkably stiff resistance. This was all compounded by poor German intelligence on their opponents' positions. There was to be no Blitzkrieg in the far north. The Germans failed to make significant gains and certainly never came close to capturing Murmansk, a "laughable" 120km (74 miles) from the German start line. After the initial effort of Silverfox, in part due to a lack of resources and in part to the passivity of their Finnish allies, the Germans in the far north shifted to defensive warfare.

THE INFLUENCE OF TERRAIN

As has been mentioned above, time and time again the terrain did not suit large-scale military operations, and this would be as good an explanation as any for the German failure in their northern offensive had not the Soviets, eventually, proved that large military operations were possible in Lapland. Nonetheless the Soviets struggled, too. The combined-arms tactics, particularly regarding the use of tanks, so painfully learned on the main fronts, did not prove particularly effective in Lapland. Swamp and, farther south, dense forest do not make good tank country. However, the Soviets did at least commit decent resources to the task. Their commander, Meretskov, had over 100,000 troops, 8000 guns and 800 planes at his disposal. Furthermore, the German position was undermined by the withdrawal of their Finnish ally. Despite this the Red Army's victory was hard won, and Rendulic, the German commander, was able to withdraw back into Norway with the bulk of his army intact.

On the whole the story of Hitler's Arctic war was a sorry one. There were bright spots: the capture of Norway was a stunning victory and accrued for Germany important strategic benefits. However, the German land campaign against Murmansk and against the Arctic convoys heading for the Soviet port were much less so. The failure to stop the convoys and, perhaps more significantly, capture Murmansk were fatal for the prospects of a German victory. The supplies of the

Western Allies contributed greatly to the USSR's ability to resist and made possible, by provision of transport and communications equipment, the great Soviet victories of 1944–45. The Germans knew this and explicitly linked the convoy battles with the war on the Eastern Front, yet German performance in the Arctic theatre was on the whole poor. Much of this was down to leadership. Dietl, the corps and subsequent army commander in Lapland, and his successor Rendulic were capable soldiers, but they were hampered by a general lack of resources. This paucity was largely down to Hitler. Such was his conviction that Norway was the "zone of destiny" and had to be defended at all costs that he refused to divert any of the huge force occupying Norway to the Arctic front. The poor performance of the Kriegsmarine against the Arctic convoys was also his fault. He overrode Raeder's sound Atlantic strategy for Germany's surface fleet. This led to its concentration in northern Norway. Once there, the fact that Hitler had no grasp of his ships' proper use and *his* real timidity when it came to naval strategy ensured the campaign was badly conducted. He enabled the Royal Navy to establish both tactical and strategic advantage over the Kriegsmarine and Luftwaffe, which in theory held all the advantages. The man who brought the war to the Arctic was also guilty of losing it there.

Red Army T-34 tanks in northern Russia. The Soviets tried to use large numbers of tanks in the Arctic, but found that they could not traverse the terrain and were restricted to the few roads, where they became prey to German anti-tank guns.

CHAPTER NOTES

Introduction

1 Lucas, James, *Hitler's Mountain Troops*, London: Arms and Armour, 1991, pp.9-10, and MacDonald, Peter, "Arctic and Mountain Warfare" in Holmes, Richard, *The Oxford Companion to Military History*, Oxford: OUP, 2001, pp.70-1.

2 See, Woodman, Richard, *Arctic Convoys, 1941–45*, London: John Murray, 1995. pp.xiv-xviii.

3 Sweden lost Finland to Russia in 1809, but under the leadership of a former marshal of Napoleon, Bernadotte, or Karl-Johan as he was known to his adopted country, managed to regain something out of the wars by capturing Norway from Denmark in 1814, the Danes stubbornly refusing to renounce their alliance with France.

4 The best one-volume history of Scandinavia is Derry, T.K., *A History of Scandinavia*, Minneapolis: University of Minnesota Press, 1979.

5 For both quotes and basis of the paragraph, see Kersaudy, Françoise, *Norway: 1940*, London: Arrow, pp.10-12.

6 This work's bibliography provides a reasonably comprehensive list of English, and some German and Scandinavian books and articles on the subject.

Chapter 1

1 Jussila, Osmo, Hentilä, Seppo and Nevakivi, Juha, *From Grand Duchy to a Modern State: A Political History of Finland since 1809*, London: Hurst, 1999, pp.104-5.

2 Kirby, David, *Finland in the Twentieth Century*, London: Hurst, 1979, p.48.

3 Screen, J.E.O., *Mannerheim: The Finnish Years*, London: Hurst, 2000, p.30.

4 Jussila et al, p.117.

5 Mannerheim, Gustaf, *Memoirs*, London: Cassell, 1953, p.159.

6 Kirby, *Finland*, p.55.

7 No less that 49 battalion members subsequently reached the rank of general officer and five, Aarne Sihvo, Erik Heinrichs, Kaarlo Heiskanen, Hugo Österman and Jarl Lundquist, served as commander-in-chief. Tillotson, H.M., *Finland at Peace and War*, Norwich: Michael Russell, appendix 1.

8 Stalin cited in Watt, D.C., *How War Came*, London: Mandarin, 1989, p.365.

9 Jussila et al, p.175.

10 In fact Yartsev's real name was Rybkin and he was the highest-ranking NKVD man at the embassy.

11 Jussila et al, p.176.

12 Eljas Erkko to the *Eduskunta*, 6 June 1939, in Watt, p.364.

13 Ribbentrop to Schulenberg,

14 August 1939 in Haslam, Jonathan, *The Soviet Union and the Struggle for Collective Security in Europe, 1933–39*, London: Macmillan, 1984, pp.226-7.

14 Mannerheim, September 1939 in Screen, p.130.

15 Kirby, *Finland*, p.123.

16 Conquest, Robert, *Stalin: Breaker of Nations*, London: Weidenfeld, 1993, p.228.

17 Jörgensen, Christer and Mann, Christopher, *Tank Warfare*, Staplehurst: Spellmount, 2001, p.38, and Upton Anthony, "Finnish-Soviet War" in Dear, I.C.B. and Foot, M.R.D., *The Oxford Companion to the Second World War*, Oxford: OUP, 1995, p.372.

18 Harvey's Diary, 24 December 1939, in Harvey, John (ed), *The Diplomatic Diaries of Oliver Harvey, 1937–40*, London: Cassell, 1970, p.332.

19 Salmon, Patrick, "British Strategy and Norway 1939–40" in Salmon, Patrick (ed), *Britain and Norway in the Second World War*, London: HMSO, 1995, p.3.

20 Hitler to Sven Hedin, 16 October 1939, in Tanner, Vaino, *The Winter War*, Stanford: Stanford UP, 1957, p.83

21 ibid, p.120.

22 Cited in Nation, Craig R., *Black Earth, Red Star: A History of Soviet Security Policy 1917–91*,

Ithaca: Cornell UP, 1992,
p.106.

23 Jörgensen and Mann, p.39.

Chapter 2

1 For a more detailed
   explanation of this argument
   see Moulton, J.L., *The
   Norwegian Campaign of 1940: A
   Study in Warfare in Three
   Dimensions*, London: Eyre and
   Spottiswoode, 1966.

2 Wegener, Wolfgang,
   Die Seestrategie des Weltkrieges,
   Berlin: 1929. See also
   Macintyre, Donald, *Narvik*,
   London: Evans, 1959, p.15.
   For Norway's attitude in World
   War I see Riste, Olav, *The
   Neutral Ally: Norway's
   relationship with Belligerent
   Powers in the First World War*,
   London: Allen and Unwin,
   1965.

3 Reflections of the C-in-C Navy
   on the outbreak of war,
   3 September 1939, and Report
   of the C-in-C Navy to the
   Führer, 10 October 1939, in *The
   Fuehrer Conferences on Naval
   Affairs, 1939–45*, Annapolis:
   Naval Institute Press, 1990,
   pp.37-8 and p.47.

4 Dahl, Hans Fredrik, *Quisling:
   A Study in Treachery*,
   Cambridge: CUP, 1999, p.155.

5 H.W. Schmidt to Admiral
   Bohemia, 31 January 1955,
   Jodl's diary, Kranke, 15 June
   1948, and deposition de

l'admiral Raeder, 17 May 1946,
cited by Kersaudy, François,
Norway, 1940, London: Arrow,
1990, pp.42-4.

6 Shirer, William L., *The Rise
   and Fall of the Third Reich*,
   London: Arrow, 1960, p.680.

7 Falkenhorst cited by Kersaudy,
   p.46.

8 Harvey, Maurice, *Scandinavian
   Misadventure: The Norwegian
   Campaign 1940*, Staplehurst:
   Spellmount, 1990,
   pp.44-5, and Goerlitz, Walter,
   *The German General Staff:
   1657–1945*, New York: Praeger,
   1953, pp.370-1

9 Harvey, p.46.

10 Perhaps the British were not so
   far wrong in this determination.
   Hitler certainly seemed to think
   so. Von Ribbentrop admitted to
   his interrogators after the war
   that when Hitler heard of
   British and French plans he
   claimed: "This would be
   disastrous for us. We have no
   more Swedish iron and all that.
   We can't go on with this war."
   Von Ribbentrop interview,
   8 October 1945 in Overy,
   Richard, *Interrogations: The
   Nazi Elite in Allied Hands, 1945*,
   London: Allen Lane, 2001,
   p.525. The best book on the
   whole iron ore issue is Munch-
   Petersen, Thomas, *The Strategy
   of Phoney War*, Stockholm:
   Militärhistoriska Förlaget,
   1981.

11 Churchill, Winston S., *The
   Gathering Storm, Volume I*,
   London: Cassell, 1948, p.463.

12 Brookes, Ewart, *Prologue to a
   War: The Navy's Part in the
   Narvik Campaign*, London:
   Jarrolds, 1966, p.30.

13 For this remarkable act the
   Glowworm's captain, the aptly
   nicknamed "Rammer" Roope,
   received a posthumous Victoria
   Cross.

14 Kersaudy, p.62.

15 Riste, Olav, "Norway" in Dear
   and Foot (eds), p.820.

16 Koht, Halvdan, *Norway,
   Neutral and Invaded*, London:
   Macmillan, 1943, pp74-5.

17 Franz Püchler cited by Lucas,
   James, *Hitler's Mountain Troops*,
   London: Arms and Armour,
   1992, p.29.

18 Accounts vary to what actually
   the Norwegians saw at
   Kristiansand, see Macintyre,
   Narvik, pp.46-7, and Adams,
   Jack, *The Doomed Expedition:
   The Campaign in Norway*,
   London: Leo Cooper, 1989,
   p.41.

19 Hooton, E.R., *Phoenix
   Triumphant: The Rise and Rise of
   the Luftwaffe*, London: Arms
   and Armour, 1994, p.222.

20 Harvey, p.194.

21 Kersaudy, p.80.

22 For the utter chaos at Namsos
   see Carton de Wiart, Adrian,
   Happy Odyssey, London:
   Jonathan Cape, 1950, p.169.

23 De Wiart, p.172, and Kersaudy, p.159.
24 Kersaudy, p.160.
25 Lucas, p.31 and Irving, David, *Hitler's War*, London: Hodder and Stoughton, 1977, p.98.
26 Lucas, p.34.
27 Ibid, p.35.

Chapter 3

1 Tillotson, H.M., *Finland at Peace and War 1918–1993*. Norwich: Michael Russell, 1993, p.179.
2 Björkman, Leif, *Sverige inför Barbarossa, 1940–1941*, Stockholm: Allmänna Förlaget, 1971, p.22.
3 Tillotson. pp.183, 189-191
4 Erickson, John, *The Road to Stalingrad*, London: Yale University Press, 1983, p.25. Tillotson, p.186.
5 Tillotson, p187.
6 Carlgren, Wilhelm M., *Svensk utrikespolitik 1939–1945*, Stockholm: Allmänna Förlaget, 1973, pp.199-210.
7 Brunila, Kai, *Finlands krig*, Stockholm: Bokorama, 1980, pp.76-77; Tillotson, p.186.
8 Ziemke, Earl F., *The German Northern Theater of Operations 1940–1945*, Washington: Dept. of US Army, 1959, pp.121-124.
9 ibid, p.125.
10 ibid, pp.127-128.
11 Lucas, *Hitler's Mountain Troops*, p.105.
12 Ruef, Karl, *Gebirgsjäger zwischen Kreta und Murmansk*, Stuttgart, 1971, p.202.

13 Lucas, pp.105, 109.
14 Brunila, pp.79-80.
15 Ruef, p.202.
16 Brunila. pp.81-82, 107.
17 Björkman, pp.53-54, 263, 351.
18 Gyllenhaal, Lars, *Slaget om Nordkalotten. Sveriges roll i tyska och allierade operationer i norr*, Lund: Histovisk Media, 1999, p.48.
19 Björkman, p.270.
20 Ziemke, p.137.
21 Lucas, p.107.
22 ibid, pp.110-112.
23 Ziemke, p.142.
24 Lucas, p.112; Ziemke, p.142.
25 Ziemke, pp.141-154.
26 Gregory, Barry, *Mountain Warfare and Arctic Warfare. From Alexander to Afghanistan*. Bath: Patrick Stephens, 1989, p.151.
27 Referred to in text as SS *Nord* to avoid confusing it with the regular Wehrmacht units.
28 Ziemke, pp.159-178.
29 ibid, p.183.
30 Järvinen, Y.A., *Kriget fortsätter. Finsk och rysk taktik under kriget 1941–1944*, Stockholm, 1951, pp.60, 63-64, 66-69, 72, 74-78.

Chapter 4

1 Järvinen, pp.207-210, 213.
2 Ziemke, p.223.
3 Gregory, p.152.
4 ibid, pp.152, 154.
5 Lucas, p.107.
6 Järvinen, pp.249-264, 290-299, 302-305.
7 Cooper, Matthew, *The Phantom War. The German struggle against Soviet Partisans 1941–1944*. London: Macdonald, 1979, pp.1-36.
8 Peoples Commissariat for Internal Affairs.
9 Smirnov claimed the village was heavily fortified and guarded by 50 Finnish troops. It was a tissue of Soviet propaganda exaggerations and downright lies.
10 Erkkilä, Veikko, *Det nedtystade kriget*, Stockholm: Hjalmarson & Högberg, 2001, pp.18, 26, 38, 42-44, 48, 50, 72, 78, 83-84, 90, 140.
11 Järvinen, pp.267-269, 271-273, 276-278, 282, 284.

Chapter 5

1 See Roskill, S.W., *The War at Sea*, London: HMSO, 1954.
2 Denham, Henry, *Inside the Nazi Ring*, New York: Homes and Meier, 1984, pp.84-5, and Kennedy, Ludovic, *Pursuit: The Sinking of the Bismarck*, London: Collins, 1974, pp.36-7.
3 Ruge, Friedrich, *Der Seekrieg: The German Navy's Story, 1939–45*, Annapolis: United States Naval Institute, 1957, p.113.
4 See Hoidal, Oddvar, *Quisling: A Study in Treason*, Oslo: Norwegian UP, 1989, p.522.
5 Roskill, *War at Sea*, II, p.143.
6 Ruge, p.205.
7 Roskill, *War at Sea*, II, p.142.
8 Ruge, p.263, and Report of the C-in-C Navy to the Führer, 13 November 1941, and Report by the Chief of Staff, Naval Staff,

Vice Admiral Fricke, on the conference with the Führer, 22 January 1942 in *Fuehrer Confrences*, pp.237, 260.

9 Van der Porten, Edward, *The German Navy in World War Two*, London: Arthur Baker, 1969, p.195.

10 Draft of Churchill's Speech, 16 February 1942, Public Record Office (PRO), PREM 3/191/2A.

11 ibid, Churchill to Ismay for the COS Committee, 25 January 1942.

12 Ultra was the British designation of intelligence gained from German radio messages enciphered on the Engima machine. Hinsley, F.H., *British Intelligence in the Second World War*, II, London: HMSO, 1981, p.210.

13 Report by C-in-C navy to the Führer, 12 March 1942, in *Fuehrer Conferences*, pp.265-6.

14 Hitler, 14 March 1942, cited by Bekker, Cajus, *Hitler's Naval War*, London: MacDonald, 1971, p.260.

15 ibid, p.264.

16 Naval Report, 2 April 1942 and Captain Meisel in Bekker, p.265, and Report by C-in-C Navy to the Führer, 13 April 1942, in *Fuehrer Conferences*, p.274.

17 Kemp, Paul, *Convoy! Drama in Arctic Waters*, London: Arms and Armour, 1993, p.43.

18 Dönitz, Karl, *Memoirs:Ten Years and Twenty Days*, London: Cassell, 1958, p.209.

19 Admiral Burroughs cited by Kemp, p.46.

20 Wittig cited by Bekker, p.269.

21 Kemp, p.51.

22 Bonham-Carter cited by Schofield, B.B., *The Arctic Convoys*, London: MacDonald and Jane's, 1977, p.40.

23 PM to Ismay for COS, 17 May 1942 in Churchill, Vol. VII, pp.236-7.

24 Tovey cited in Woodman, Richard, *Arctic Convoys, 1941–45*, London: John Murray, 1994, p.159.

25 Dönitz cited in Schofield, p.46.

26 Roskill, *The Navy at War, 1939–45*, London: Collins, 1960, p.206.

27 Report on Conference between C-in-C Navy and the Führer, 15 June 1942, in *Fuehrer Conferences*, p.284.

28 Hinsley, II, p.217.

29 For varying versions of this decision see Schofield, p.56, Woodman, pp.213-5, Roskill, *War at Sea*, II, pp.139-40, and Peter Kemp, "Dudley Pound" in Howarth, Stephen (ed), *Men of War*, London: Weidenfeld and Nicolson, 1992, p.35.

30 Schniewind cited in Bekker, p.279.

31 Commander Reinicke to Heinz Assman and Günther Schultz cited in Bekker, pp.278-279.

32 Woodman, p.262.

33 Hughes and unnamed American ensign in Bekker, p.268.

34 Kemp, p.106.

35 Woodman, p.276.

36 Hitler cited in Bekker, p.280.

37 Raeder cited in Bekker, p.292.

38 Conference between C-in-C Navy and Führer, 26 February 1942, in *Fuehrer Conferences*, pp.311-2.

39 Barry to Alexander, 2 Febraury 1944, PRO, PREM 3/191/1.

40 Conference between the C-in-C Navy and Führer, 24 September, 1943 in *Fuehrer Conferences*, p.369, and German Navy War Diary cited in No1098/Sm04351, Final Report on Operation Source, 26 July 1945, PRO, ADM 199/888.

41 Roskill, *War at Sea*, III, *Part 2*, p.78 and Conference between C-in-C Navy and the Führer, 19 and 20 December 1943 in *Fuehrer Conferences*, p.374.

42 Busch, Fritz-Otto, *The Drama of the* Scharnhorst, London: Robert Hale, 1956, p.54.

43 CB 3081(17) Battle Summary No 24, Sinking of the *Scharnhorst*, 26 January 1943, PRO, Adm 1/15691.

44 Bey cited by Bekker, p.343.

45 Minutes of the visit of the C-in-C Navy to Wolfsschanze, 1-3 January 1944 in *Fuehrer Conferences*, p.379.

46 Conference between C-in-C navy and the Führer, 12-13 April 1944 in ibid, pp.388-9.

47 No210/9/8, Operation Mascot, 25 July 1944, PRO ADM 1/942.

48 Senior British Naval Officer to 5 Group, 16 September, 1944, PRO, AIR 14/1970.

49 The Sinking of the *Tirpitz*, 12 November 1944, NID 24/T 34/45, 1 September 1945, PRO, ADM 199/735, and Conference between C-in-C Navy and Führer 12-13 April 1944, and Conference of C-in-C at Führer headquarters, 31 October–2 November 1944 in *Fuehrer Conferences*, pp.388-9 and p.415.

50 Andrew Lambert, "Seizing the Initiative: the Arctic convoys 1944–45" in Rodger, N.A.M.(ed), *Naval Power in the 20th Century*, London Macmillan, 1996, p.160.

51 ibid, p.152.

52 Dönitz cited by Bekker, p.300.

53 Ruge, pp.284-5.

54 Gretton, P., "Former Naval Person", 1968, p.302, cited in Lambert, p.161.

Chapter 6

1 Brunila, pp.119-120.

2 Ziemke, pp.233-234.

3 ibid, p.247.

4 Brunila, p.120.

5 Ziemke, pp.272-277.

6 Nikel is the Russian name for the mining town.

7 Gregory, p.159.

8 Peter Krosby, *Finland, Germany and the Soviet Union, 1940-1941. The Petsamo Dispute*. London: University of Wisconsin Press, 1968, pp.191, 193, 195, 197-198.

9 Upton in Purnell. Vol. 20, pp.2142-2143.

10 They proved equally effective on the Arctic Front during the Soviet offensive in October.

11 Upton. Purnell. Vol. 20, pp.2143-2148.

12 Ziemke, p.292. Hitler also wanted Sweden to continue its supplies of ball bearings and iron ore, which were even more vital for German armaments production than Finnish nickel from Petsamo.

13 Hitler was aware that in 1918 the German landing in Finland and outbreak of the Finnish Civil War provoked the otherwise timorous Swedes to send troops to Aland to secure the archipelago and its population from either Russian, German or Red Finnish violence.

14 He had been killed in an aircraft accident earlier in 1944.

15 Rendulic was Austrian and had seen action during the Moscow campaign, before seeing service in Yugoslavia fighting the partisans.

16 Gebhardt, James F., *The Petsamo-Kirkenes Operation: Soviet Breakthrough and Pursuit in the Arctic*, October 1944. Fort Leavenworth: Leavenworth Papers No 17, 1990, pp.6-9.

17 Ziemke. p.302.

18 Abbreviated in the text as LRC.

19 An infantry division in the Red Army was called a Rifle Division, and by 1944 those units that had an especially impressive track record were made Guards formations, which meant being given better rations and other such perks.

20 Gebhardt, pp.11-15, 20, 23-24.

21 Tanks stuck on roads could only fire at the enemy one at a time, and proved sitting ducks for German anti-tank gunners.

22 Gebhardt, pp.31-33, 35-36, 38-45,47-62, 65-67, 69, 72-74, 76-79, 81-83; Gamst, Thorbein, *Finmark under hakekorset. "Festung Finnmark"*, Oslo: Agdin, 1984, pp.186-188, 190-191, 193, 197, 199.

23 Ziemke, p.276.

Chapter 7

1 Jodl was also convinced of Hitler's leadership ability. After the war he commented that: "One of his [Hitler's] biggest leadership achievements was the decision to occupy Norway. Interview, 29 June 1945 in Overy, *Interrogations*, p.279.

2 Report by Naval Chief of Staff, Vice Admiral Fricke on conference with the Führer, 22 January 1942, in *Fuehrer Conferences*, p.260.

3 Dahl, pp.180 and 190-1.

4 Andenæs, Johannes, Riste, Olav and Skodvin, Magne, *Norway and the Second World War*, Oslo: Aschehoug, 1966, pp.96-7.

5 See Mann, Christopher, "The Norwegian Army in Exile", in Bennett, Matthew, and Latawski, Paul (eds), *Armies in Exile*, London: Macmillan, 2002.

6 Quisling to Terboven cited in Dahl, p.244.

7 Terboven cited by Littlejohn, David, *The Patriotic Traitors*, London: Heinemann, 1972,

p.36.

8   Riste in Dear and Foot (eds), p.819.

9   Fritt Folk, 13 January 1941 cited by Andenæs, Riste and Skodvin, p.74.

10 The quote that "disappeared into the maelstrom" is from Andenæs, Riste and Skodvin, p.75. See also Littlejohn, pp.25-32 and pp.42-6, and Ohto Manninen "Operation Barbarossa and the Nordic Countries" in Nissen, Henrik (ed), *Scandinavia during the Second World War*, Oslo: Universitetforlaget, 1983, pp.176-9, and Lucas, *Mountain Troops*, pp.104-38.

11 Dahl, pp.338-9, Riste, Olav and Nøkleby, Berit, *Norway, 1940–45: The Resistance Movement*, Oslo: Aschehoug, 1970, pp.72-75.

12 For a first account see Sonsteby, Gunnar, *Report from No 24*, London: 4 Square, 1965, pp.104-8.

13 See Derry, T.K., *A History of Scandinavia*, Minneapolis: University of Minnesota Press, pp.342-4, and Nissen, Henrik "Adjusting to German Domination" in Nissen (ed), pp.132-7.

14 Foot, M.R.D., *SOE: The Special Operations Executive, 1940–45*, London: BBC, 1984, p.211, but for alternative views see Weale, Adrian, *Secret Warfare*, London: Coronet, 1997, p.79, and Grimnes, Ole Kristian "Allied Heavy Water Operations at Rjukan", IFS Info, No 4, 1996, p.10.

15 Hitler cited in Butler, J.R.M., *Grand Strategy, III, part II*, London: HMSO, 1964, p.500.

16 Liddell Hart Centre for Military Archives, Alanbrooke papers, *Notes on My Life*, Vol. V, p.403.

17 Morgan, Fredrick, *Peace and War*, London: Hodder and Stoughton, 1961, p.175.

18 It is worth noting, however – although there is some debate about this – that by chance the British captured code wheels for the Enigma machine in the first Lofoten raid. This was a gain of real strategic import. See Kahn, David, *Seizing the Enigma*, London: Arrow, 1992, pp.127-37.

19 Butler, p.500.

20 Einar Grannes, "Operation Jupiter: A Norwegian Perspective", in Salmon (ed), p.114.

21 Masterman, John, *The Double-Cross System in the War of 1939–45*, London: Pimlico, 1972, p.130.

22 On the significance of Thorne see Howard, Michael, *Strategic Deception in the Second World War*, London: Pimlico, 1989, p.111, and also Thorne, Peter, "Hitler and the Gheluvet Article", *Guards Magazine*, Autumn, 1987, pp.106-7, and Hart, Stephen, "The Forgotten Liberator: The 1939–45 Military Career of General Sir Andrew Thorne", *Journal of the Society for Army Historical records*, No 319, Autumn 2001, p.243.

23 FHW assessment in Howard, p.117.

24 Norges Hjemmefrontmuseum, Wilson, John, *SOE Norwegian Section History, 1941–45*, unpublished, 1945, p143.

25 Böhme cited by Hauge, Jens-Christain, *The Liberation of Norway*, Oslo: Gyldendal, 1995, p.91.

26 PRO, WO 106/1985, GON 111, Garner-Smith to Stockdale, 26 May 1945.

27 Støren cited by Andenæs, Riste and Skodvin, p.81.

Conclusion

1   See above Chapter 3 and Lucas, p.105.

2   Report of the Chief of the Naval Staff on conference with the Führer, 22 January 1942, in *Fuerhrer Conferences*, p.261.

3   See Ziemke, Earl, "German-Soviet War" in Dear and Foot (eds), p.434.

4   For the best exposition of these arguments see Van Dyke, Carl, *The Soviet Invasion of Finland, 1939–40*, London: Frank Cass, 1997, and for the Soviet discussions in the aftermath of the conflict see Chubaryan, Alexander and Shukman, Harold (eds), *Stalin and the Soviet-Finnish War, 1939–40*, London: Frank Cass, 2002.

5   Screen, pp.173-5 and Upton, Anthony, *Finland in Crisis: 1940–44*, London: Faber, 1964, p.267.

BIBLIOGRAPHY

ARCHIVAL SOURCES

ADM 1 – Admiralty and Secretariat Papers

ADM 199 – Admiralty War History Cases and Papers

AIR 14 – RAF Bomber Command Papers

Liddell Hart Centre for Military Archives, King's College, London

Alanbrooke papers

PREM 3 – Prime Minister's Operational Correspondence and Papers

Norges Hjemmefrontmuseum, Oslo

Public Record Office (PRO), Kew, London

Wilson, John, SOE Norwegian Section History, 1941-45, unpublished, 1945.

WO 106 – War Office: Military Headquarters Papers: Home Forces, 1939-45

DOCUMENTS, MEMOIRS AND DIARIES

The Fuehrer Conferences on Naval Affairs, 1939–45, Annapolis: Naval Institute Press, 1990

Carton de Wiart, Adrian, Happy Odyssey, London: Jonathan Cape, 1950

Chubaryan, Alexander and Shukman, Harold, (eds) Stalin and the Soviet Finnish War, 1939–40, London: Frank Cass, 2002

Churchill, Winston S., The Gathering Storm, I, London: Cassell, 1948

Denham, Henry, Inside the Nazi Ring, New York: Homes and Meier, 1984

Dönitz, Karl, Memoirs: Ten Years and Twenty Days, London: Cassell, 1958

Gripenberg, G.A., Finland and the Great Powers, Lincoln: University of Nebraska Press, 1965

Harvey, John (ed) The Diplomatic Diaries of Oliver Harvey, 1937–40, Cassell: London, 1970

Hauge, Jens-Christian, The Liberation of Norway, Oslo: Gyldendal, 1995

Koht, Halvdan, Norway, Neutral and Invaded, London: Macmillan, 1943

Lie, Trygve, Kampen for Norges Frihet, 1940–45, Oslo: Borregaard, 1958

Mannerheim, Gustaf, Memoirs, Cassell: London, 1953,

Masterman, John, The Double-Cross System in the War of 1939–45, London: Pimlico, 1972

Morgan, Fredrick, Peace and War, London: Hodder and Stoughton, 1961

Sontag, Raymond and Beddie, James, (eds), Nazi-Soviet Relations, 1939–41: Documents from the Archives of the German Foreign Office, Westport: Greenwood, 1976

Tanner, Vaino, The Winter War, Stanford: Stanford UP, 1957

BOOKS

Adams, Jack, The Doomed Expedition: The Campaign in Norway, London: Leo Cooper, 1989

Andenæs, Johannes, Riste, Olav and Skodvin, Magne, Norway and the Second World War, Oslo: Aschehoug, 1966

Ash, Bernard, Norway: 1940, London: Cassell, 1964

Bekker, Cajus, Hitler's Naval War, London: MacDonald, 1971

Bennett, Matthew and Latawski, Paul (eds), Armies in Exile, London: Macmillan, 2002

Blyth, J.D.M, The War in Arctic Europe, London, 1945

Björkman, Leif, Sverige inför Operation Barbarossa. Svensk neutralitetspolitik 1940–1941, Stockholm: Allmänna Förlaget, 1971

Borgersrud, Lars, Unngå å Irritere Fienden, Oslo: Oktober, 1981.

Brett-Smith, Richard, Hitler's Generals, San Rafael: Presidio Press, 1977

Brookes, Ewart, Prologue to a War: The Navy's Part in the Narvik Campaign, London: Jarrolds, 1966

Brunila, Kai, Finlands krig, Stockholm: Bokorama, 1980

Busch, Fritz-Otto, The Drama of the Scharnhorst, London: Robert Hale, 1956

Butler, J.R.M., Grand Strategy, III, Part II, London: HMSO, 1964

Claasen, Adam, Hitler's Northern War: The Luftwaffe's Ill-fated Campaign, 1940–45, Lawrence: UP of Kansas, 2001

Clark, Douglas, Three Days to Catastrophe, London: Hammond and Hammond, 1966

Condon, Richard, The Winter War, London: Ballantine, 1972

Conquest, Robert, Stalin: Breaker of Nations, London: Weidenfeld, 1993

Dahl, Hans Fredrik, Quisling: A Study in Treachery, Cambridge: CUP, 1999

Dahl, H.F., Hjeltnes, G., Nokleby, B., Ringdal, N.J. and Sorensen, Oystein, Norsk Krigsleksikon, 1940–45, Oslo: J.W. Cappelens, 1995

Dear, I.C.B. and Foot, M.R.D. (eds) The Oxford Companion to the Second World War, Oxford: OUP, 1995

Deighton, Len, Blitzkrieg, London: Grafton, 1981

Derry, T.K., *A History of Scandinavia*, Minneapolis: University of Minnesota Press, 1979

Engle, Eloise and Paananen, Lauri, *The Winter War*, London: Sidgwick and Jackson, 1973

Erkkilä, Veikko, *Det nedtystade kriget. När sovjetiska partisaner anföll finska gränsbyar*, Stockholm: Hjalmarson & Höberg, 2001

Foot, M.R.D., *SOE: The Special Operations Executive, 1940–45*, London: BBC, 1984

Gebhardt, James F., *The Petsamo-Kirkenes Operation: Soviet Breakthrough and Pursuit in the Arctic, October 1944*, Fort Leavenworth (Kansas): Leavenworth Papers No.17, 1990

Goerlitz, Walter, *The German General Staff: 1657–1945*, New York: Praeger, 1953,

Gregory, Barry, *Mountain and Arctic Warfare. From Alexander to Afghanistan*, London: Patrick Stephens, 1989

Gyllenhaal, Lars and Gebhardt, James F., *Slaget om Nordkalotten*, Lund: Histovisk Media, 1999

Harvey, Maurice, *Scandinavian Misadventure: The Norwegian Campaign 1940*, Staplehurst: Spellmount, 1990

Haslam, Jonathan, *The Soviet Union and the Struggle for Collective Security in Europe, 1933–39*, London: Macmillan, 1984

Hinsley, F.H., *British Intelligence in the Second World War*, London: HMSO, 1981

Hoidal, Oddvar, *Quisling: A Study in Treason*, Oslo: Norwegian UP, 1989

Holmes, Richard, (ed), *The Oxford Companion to Military History*, Oxford: OUP, 2001

Hölter, Hermann, *Armee in der Arktis: die Operationen der deutschen Lappland-Armee*, Munich, 1977

Hooton, E.R., *Phoenix Triumphant: The Rise and Rise of the Luftwaffe*, London: Arms and Armour, 1994

Howard, Michael, *Strategic Deception in the Second World War*, London: Pimlico, 1989

Howarth, Stephen (ed), *Men of War*, London: Weidenfeld and Nicolson, 1992,

Irving, David, *Hitler's War*, London: Hodder and Stoughton, 1977

Jörgensen, Christer and Mann, Christopher, *Tank Warfare*, Staplehurst: Spellmount, 2001

Jussila, Osmo, Hentilä, Seppo and Nevakivi, Juha, *From Grand Duchy to a Modern State: A Political History of Finland since 1809*, London: Hurst, 1999

Kahn, David, *Seizing the Enigma*, London: Arrow, 1992

Kemp, Paul, *Convoy! Drama in Arctic Waters*, London: Arms and Armour, 1993

Kennedy, Ludovic, *Pursuit: The Sinking of the Bismarck*, London: Collins, 1974,

Kersaudy, Françoise, *Norway: 1940*, London: Arrow, 1990

Littlejohn, David, *The Patriotic Traitors*, London: Heinemann 1972

Kirby, David, *Finland in the Twentieth Century*, London: Hurst, 1979

Krosby, Hans P., *Finland, Germany and the Soviet Union, 1940–1941. The Petsamo Dispute*, London: University of Wisconsin Press, 1968

Laqueur, Walter, *Russia and Germany: A Century of Conflict*, London: Weidenfeld and Nicolson, 1965

Liddell Hart, *The Other Side of the Hill*, London: Pan, 1951

Lucas, James, *Hitler's Mountain Troops*, London: Arms and Armour, 1991,

Macintyre, Donald, *Narvik*, London: Evans, 1959,

Mitchell, Donald W., *A History of Russian and Soviet Sea Power*, London: Cassell, 1974

Moulton, J.L., *The Norwegian Campaign of 1940: A Study in Warfare in Three Dimensions*, London: Eyre and Spottiswoode, 1966

Munch-Petersen, Thomas, *The Strategy of Phoney War*, Stockholm: Militärhistoriska Förlaget, 1981

Nation, R. Craig, Black Earth, Red Star: *A History of Soviet Security Policy 1917–91*, Ithaca: Cornell UP, 1992,

Nissen, Henrik (ed), *Scandinavia during the Second World War*, Oslo: Universitetforlaget, 1983

Osborn, Patrick, *Operation Pike: Britain versus the Soviet Union, 1939–41*, Westport: Greenwood, 2000

Overy, Richard, *Interrogations: The Nazi Elite in Allied Hands, 1945*, London: Allen Lane, 2001

Petrow, Richard, *The Bitter Years*, London: Purnell, 1974

Ries, Tomas, *Cold Will: The Defence of Finland*, London: Brassey's, 1988

Riste, Olav, *Londons-regjeringa: Norge I krigsalliansen, 1940–45*, I–II, 1973-79

Riste, Olav, *The Neutral Ally: Norway's relationship with Belligerent Powers in the First World War*, London: Allen and Unwin, 1965

Riste, Olav and Nøkleby, Berit, *Norway, 1940–45: The Resistance Movement*, Oslo: Aschehoug, 1970

Rodger, N.A.M.(ed), *Naval Power in the 20th Century*, London: Macmillan, 1996

Roskill, S.W., *The Navy at War, 1939–45*, London: Collins 1960

Roskill, S.W., *The War at Sea, I,II and III*, London: HMSO, 1954-61

Ruef, Karl, *Gebirgsjäger zwischen Kreta und Murmansk: die Shicksale der 6 Gebrigsdivision*, Graz, 1970

Ruge, Friedrich, *Der Seekrieg: The German Navy's Story, 1939–45*, Annapolis: United States Naval Institute, 1957

Salmon, Patrick (ed), *Britain and Norway in the Second World War*, London: HMSO, 1995

Schofield, B.B., *The Arctic Convoys*, London: MacDonald and Jane's, 1977

Screen, J.E.O., *Mannerheim: The Finnish Years*, London: Hurst, 2000

Shirer, William L., *The Rise and Fall of the Third Reich*, London: Arrow, 1960,

Sonsteby, Gunnar, *Report from No 24*, London: 4 Square, 1965

Steen, Sverre (ed) *Norges Krig, I-III*, Oslo: Gylendal, 1947-50

Tarrrant, V.E., *The Last Year of the Kriegsmarine*, London: Arms and Armour, 1994

Thorban, F.W., *Der Abwehrkampfen um Petsamo und Kirkenes 1944. Operation Birke und Nordlicht. Die letzte Schlackt an der Eismeerfront im oktober 1944*, Friedberg, 1989

Tillotson, H.M., *Finland at Peace and War*, Norwich: Michael Russell, 1993

Upton, Anthony, *Finland in Crisis: 1940–4*, London: Faber, 1964

Van der Porten, Edward, *The German Navy in World War Two*, London: Arthur Baker, 1969

Van Dyke, Carl, *The Soviet Invasion of Finland, 1939–40*, London: Frank Casss, 1997

Watt, D.C., *How War Came*, London: Mandarin, 1989

Weale, Adrian, *Secret Warfare*, London: Coronet, 1997

Wegener, Wolfgang, *Die Seestrategie des Weltkrieges*, Berlin: 1929

Woodman, Richard, *Arctic Convoys, 1941–45*, London: John Murray, 1995

Ziemke, Earl F, *The German Northern Theater of Operations 1940–1945*, Washington: Dept. of US Army, 1959

ARTICLES

Corum, James, "The German Campaign in Norway 1940 as a Joint Operation", *Journal of Strategic Studies*, Vol 21, No 4, 1998

Dietrich Loock, H., "Weserübung: A Step towards the Greater German Reich", *Scandinavian Journal of History*, No 2, 1977

Grannes, Einar, "Operation Jupiter: A Norwegian Perspective" in Salmon, Patrick (ed), *Britain and Norway in the Second World War*, London: HMSO, 1995

Grimnes, Ole Kristian "Allied Heavy Water Operations at Rjukan", *IFS Info*, No 4, 1996

Hart, Stephen, "The Forgotten Liberator: The 1939–45 Military Career of General Sir Andrew Thorne", *Journal of the Society for Army Historical Records*, No 319, Autumn 2001

Lambert, Andrew, "Seizing the Initiative: the Arctic convoys 1944–45", in Rodger, N.A.M.(ed), *Naval Power in the 20th Century*, London: Macmillan, 1996

Mann, Christopher, "The Norwegian Army in Exile", in Matthew Bennett and Paul Latawski (eds), *Armies in Exile*, London: Macmillan, 2002

Nissen, Henrik, "Adjusting to German Domination", in Nissen, Henrik (ed), *Scandinavia during the Second World War*, Oslo: Universitetforlaget, 1983

Parker, R.A.C., "Britain, France and Scandinavia, 1939–40", *History*, Vol 61, 1976

Salmon, Patrick, "British Strategy and Norway 1939–40", in Salmon, Patrick (ed), *Britain and Norway in the Second World War*, London: HMSO, 1995

Manninen, Ohto, "Operation Barbarossa and the Nordic Countries", in Nissen, Henrik (ed), *Scandinavia during the Second World War*, Oslo: Universitetforlaget, 1983

Thompson, David, "Norwegian Military Policy, 1905–40: A Critical Appraisal and Review of the Literature", *Journal of Military History*, Vol 61, No 7, 1997

Thorne, Peter, "Hitler and the Gheluvet Article", *Guards Magazine*, Autumn, 1987

Upton, Anthony F., "Barbarossa: The Finnish Front June–December 1941", *Purnell's History of the Second World War* Vol 6, London, 1980

Upton, Anthony F., "The End of the Arctic War June–October 1944", *Purnell's History of the Second World War*, Vol 20, London, 1981

INDEX

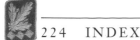